Beyond Paper

Beyond Paper

the official guide to
Adobe™ Acrobat™

Patrick Ames
Foreword by **John Warnock**

Adobe Press
Mountain View
California

Patents Pending.

Library of Congress Catalog Number **93-78061**

ISBN 0-56830-050-6

First Printing June 1993
10 9 8 7 6 5 4 3 2

Printed in the United States of America. Published simultanously in Canada.

Published and distributed by Hayden Books, a division of Prentice Hall Computer Publishing. For sales and corporate sales information contact: Prentice Hall Computer Publishing, 1-800-428-5331, or address Hayden Books, 11711 North College Avenue, Carmel, IN 46032.

A major university library is spending $1.5 million on a supercomputer to electronically store the contents of more than 40,000 deteriorating old books. The cost of building a library addition to house those books would be $20 million.

FOREWORD

We live in a sea of paper. Our everyday lives are flooded with newspapers, magazines, catalogues, promotional pieces, forms, and all manner of other printed communication. Information is exploding at a rate that is pushing the boundaries of our abilities to cope with it. Trees are being used up in ever-increasing numbers. Energy costs for shipping paper is increasing. The basic infrastructure and environment linked to our use of paper is straining to the point of collapse.

Look at paper's growth curve beginning in the 1800s and watch it climb with each technical advance – the invention of Linotype and Monotype machines, the improvements in typesetting, phototypesetting, production facilities, and now, the personal computer and desktop publishing – the paper curve is off the graph. If this curve is extrapolated into the future, no matter how much recycling we do or how much we try to reuse paper resources, it simply isn't going to work. The growth rate far exceeds the supply of trees.

Calculate how much it costs to transport paper across the United States or across the world, and how much over night mail costs, and how many hundreds of millions of pieces of mail the post office handles. Look just at the energy it takes to transport all that paper from point to point, or the employee hours needed to process and shuffle all that information. The conclusion is the same:

it simply isn't going to work. Ninety-nine percent of the information, at least that I get, goes into the circular file. I don't have an opportunity to read it because there is too much of it to carry around, and I don't have a spare room large enough to store it, and if I did, I still wouldn't have an efficient way to retrieve it.

The current computer environment is our last best solution. Computer systems are becoming more and more powerful and computer memory less and less expensive. Business and government are beginning to build wide-area and local-area networks, a digital highway capable of moving and storing information. These networks, however, have only the most fundamental kind of electronic mail systems; no document with anything more complex than ASCII text can be transmitted. As well, communication among our most advanced and powerful computers just doesn't work: we all own different kinds of computers and they are unable to talk to one another.

▶ *page 119*

Should I make my entire corporation conform to one kind of operating system with one set of applications? Can I achieve uniformity within my own business? Neither question has an answer because every organization works differently, even under the same corporate or government umbrella. Employees say, "I want a Macintosh for desktop publishing; or, I want to put my financial systems on a PC;

or, I want to do my engineering work on a UNIX workstation." All of these platforms have legitimate advantages for the type of computing done on them, but as communications tools they don't work. Information still can't be sent from computer system to computer system, and that basically means information can't be shared within a business, and sometimes, between businesses.

When you pick up the phone, you don't ask what kind of phone the person on the other end is using. Phones communicate to other phones. When you produce an electronic document, you shouldn't have to think about where it's going, or what applications or which fonts are being used. You should just be able to send it and share it.

Most documents are created for basic informational purposes, not for someone else to edit. When I get financial reports from my CFO in the form of spreadsheets, I don't edit those spreadsheets; I look at the information. When I get *Business Week* in the mail, I'm not tempted to edit it, and I'm not interested in editing the majority of memos and proposals I receive.

Computers create information but they don't communicate it, and that is the computer's inherent flaw.

This entire set of problems is what Adobe Systems addresses with Adobe™ Acrobat™. We've already begun using Acrobat technology inside of Adobe. I can now put a document onto a file server and not worry about whether people's computers can open it or print it, or whether it has all the right fonts. It changes the way we work, and the way we think about communication.

The Adobe Acrobat family of products is a set of tools we think will solve the problem of cross-platform communication of documents, and the communication of documents for informational purposes. You can now capture specific information from your marketing report and publish it to the rest of your company.

The amazing thing about Acrobat technology is that you don't have to do anything special to use it. You don't have to change any of your environments, or alter your hardware, software, or network configurations. Adobe has learned that to change the way people work, or change people's computing behavior, the transition process has to be as easy as possible. We've learned that if the technology is easy to adopt, then it is readily accepted.

We've removed the obstacles that make people avoid new technology. Acrobat technology is operating-system independent, viewable on all platforms, and printable on all printers. A PostScript printer isn't necessary: an ink jet printer will print the image and the type for you. If you have a fax hook-up, Acrobat software will work as well.

 pages 36-43

Acrobat software has text searching, as well. One of the most glaring deficiencies in technologies that capture page images (fax, for example) is the inability to retain text information and to search the documents.

pages
115-117

Files created with Acrobat technology are searchable, and the structure is completely extensible, meaning that Adobe has a commitment to advance the technology even further in both the near and distant future. What Adobe, and this book, is saying is that we now have an opportunity to change the way we work for the better.

We hope you will use Adobe Acrobat software and accomplish things our engineers and all the others at Adobe never thought could be done beyond paper. It's that simple. It's that compelling.

JOHN E. WARNOCK
CEO, Adobe Systems Incorporated

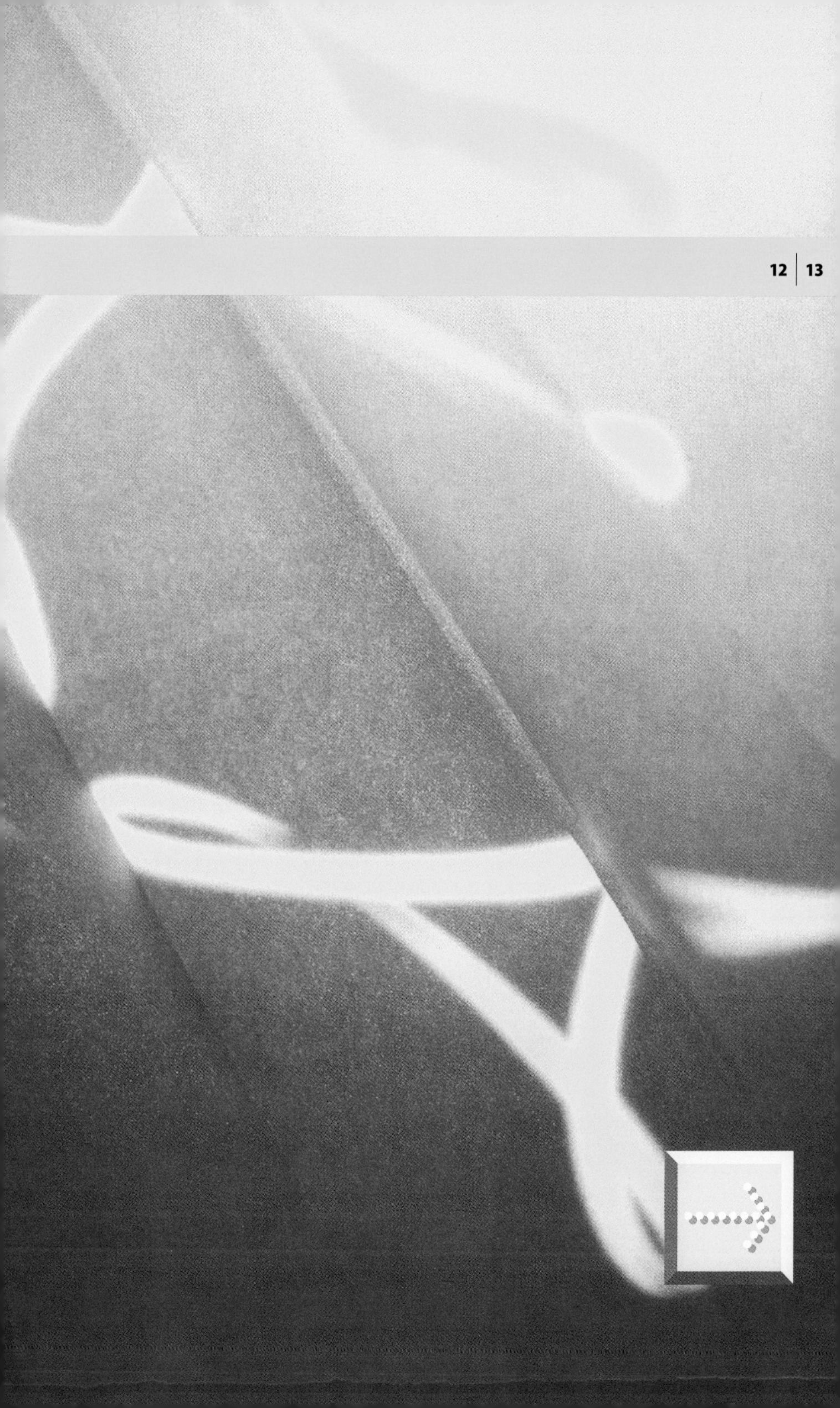

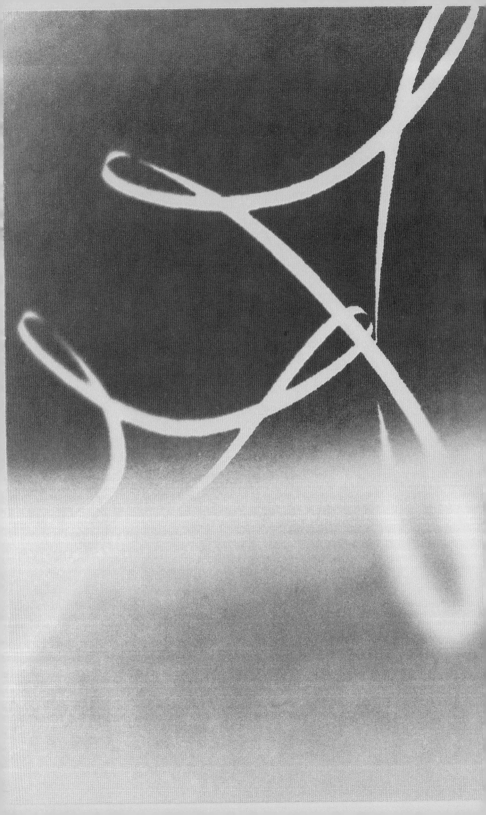

Beyond Paper

A law office employing 60 attorneys estimates that it uses 65,000 pounds of paper a month, or more than 1,000 pounds per attorney.

INTRODUCTION

When you receive a document you are expected to do something with it – print it, share it, read it, file it, copy it, archive it, or like many documents, discard it.

It is this document processing that occupies the businesses, governments, and institutions of the world each and every day to the extent that employees spend up to 60 percent of their time processing documents.

With the advent of the personal computer many experts believed a "paperless" office would alleviate this document processing, but we tend only to create more elaborate, and often better-looking documents, not paperless documents. Technology has provided better document creation tools, not better document processing tools. We still distribute paper documents in traditional, time-consuming, and expensive ways – by hand.

Adobe™ Acrobat™ software offers an alternative method of processing and distributing documents in a unique and robust way by combining the promise of digital information with the traditional security of printed materials.

Most people cannot objectively assess their own document processing routines. Most people do not believe there is any "problem" to be solved – they get their work done and their documents processed. What *Beyond Paper* attempts to do is analyze today's document processing habits and show how the Adobe Acrobat technology can improve communication, speed distribution, and create intelligent information that can be manipulated, accessed, searched, and stored electronically.

Beyond Paper is organized into the hours of a normal business day. Each hour constitutes a chapter, and each chapter has a different type of document as its theme. The chapters create a before and after case study of how documents are created and processed today, and then how things might be different using Acrobat software. Each chapter has an ending section, a how-to section, that describes how various Adobe Acrobat products are used to achieve the results mentioned within the chapter's case study. Following the theme of the normal business day, two coffee breaks and a lunch break chapter are meant to educate and entertain.

Our day is spend at two workplaces: the morning with CubeWorks, a 350-employee manufacturer of office partitions and furnishings; the afternoon with the Bythos Corporation, a packaged-food conglomerate with over 15,000 employees worldwide. At 5:00 pm, we conclude the day with a brief look at future Adobe Acrobat products that address commercial publishing tools: food for thought on your commute ride home.

Beyond Paper does not attempt to re-hash product documentation of Adobe Acrobat software, or present page after page of how-tos or tips and techniques: Acrobat software is surprisingly easy to use and quick to learn. Using case studies modeled after real-life situations, this book will trigger the imagination for using Acrobat technology to improve and simplify the way you work.

If you work in an office and use a computer to create documents that other people read, this book will help you understand the workflow benefits of Adobe Acrobat software.

 pages 115-117

The Presentation
Converting a document from one application format to another is easy when your entire staff stops what they're doing to help for a day or two.

Navigating and maneuvering through electronic documents with Acrobat Exchange.

Lunch: Acrobat Reader and Acrobat Exchange
Comparing the two application versions of the Acrobat viewing engine.

The Morning Memo
The memo, the most common form of written communication, requires more time to distribute than it does to create. What's the best way to get those documents to Seattle?

How to create PDF files using PDF Writer.

| 8:00 am | 9:00 am | 10:00 am | 11:00 am | noon |

Coffee Break
The cost of processing and distributing all those paper documents can be enormous, but have you given any thought to staples, binders, and scissors?

The Diverse Document
Creating a document from pieces of other documents can eat up a good chunk of the day. Have you read the user's manual on your copier?

Creating a new and exciting Acrobat document from one that is plain and ordinary can enliven even the dullest work day.

The Project Proposal
If you want feedback on your proposals before a meeting don't send them via interoffice mail. And don't ever follow the mailboy about on his rounds.

Viewing documents on the screen with Acrobat Exchange: Windows, Macintosh, DOS , UNIX.

Complex Documents in a Complex Environment
Twenty barrels of vanilla, a truckload of sugar, and twenty-two hundred egg yolks will cost you about the same as mass-producing the document for its recipe.

After a pop quiz the real answers to font substitution.

The Portable Document
Mobile computing takes on a whole new meaning with portable documents. Documents that live their entire lives electronically are documents able to keep the pace of modern life.

1:00 PM · **2:00 PM** · **3:00 PM** · **4:00 PM** · **5:00 PM**

Coffee Break
Acrobat can speed along even those memos that backfire on your career.
So go ahead, send them and duck.

Tomorrow's Document
Future Adobe Acrobat technology including structured documents, OCR technology, search engines, and commercial publishing.

The Internal Document
The cost of internal corporate documents is not an employee benefit. Accessing the information is.

Creating PDF files using the network accessible Acrobat Distiller program.

The Interactive Document
Information can be presented in any number of ways: linearly, intuitively, or interactively. Acrobat technology gives you the option to do all three in the same electronic document.

Show and tell it interactively.

A commission set up by the US Congress
recommends that US businesses set a goal
to increase productivity 2% each year.
For the past twenty years the average has been about .08%.

THE SIMPLE MEMO

8:00^{am}

Elizabeth James, Chief Executive Officer of CubeWorks, an office partition and furniture manufacturer, will soon begin another day in the eight-year life of her company of 350 talented and dedicated employees, a company she built with hard work and an astute business sense.

Despite Elizabeth's inspired leadership CubeWorks is coping with an ever-changing business world where the marketplace demands better products at lower prices.

CubeWorks has taken all the traditional steps to "down-size" the business to effect a profitable operation. Elizabeth and her management staff trimmed costs wherever they could: salary increases are carefully monitored and bonuses no longer exist; new hires need Elizabeth's direct approval; computer and software purchases must be authorized by VP-level signatures; and, all travel expenditures must have prior managerial approval.

While progress has been made it has left CubeWorks threadbare of personnel resources: 1.5 workers do what was once done by 2 workers. Efficiencies of scale have made everyone's workday busy, if not hectic.

CubeWorks begins its day in the same competitive climate as other businesses and institutions all over the world. Large or small, manufacturing or service, corporate or private, government or educational, the day begins with people communicating information to each other. The more critical that information is, the more timely and useful the communication should be.

One potential area of savings CubeWorks has not examined is the most obvious and common part of their business day – how they process and distribute information.

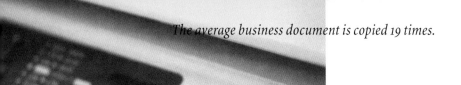

THE SIMPLE MEMO

When Elizabeth arrives at her office, she skims her calendar, leafs through a stack of mail, and then reaches for the phone to listen to her voice mail messages. One, two, three messages, and then number four. The Zeb Group, an investment brokerage firm, has leased the entire downtown City Center office complex. John Zeb wants to meet with Elizabeth and her staff next week to discuss the complete retrofitting of City Center for its 3,000 employees.

Elizabeth quickly returns the call, confirming a meeting for next week. She considers what to do, how to move, and who needs to be informed – this is an opportunity that cannot be squandered.

Elizabeth decides to write an official memo to all employees. She begins writing an E-mail memo but soon discovers it looks like every other memo on the computer bulletin board. Besides, she wants to use graphs to detail the current financial status of the company, but E-mail cannot incorporate the computer-generated graphs. She re-writes the memo in a word processing application and electronically pastes in the graphs.

E-mail systems deliver information only in ASCII text. They are incapable of delivering documents that have formatting, graphics, or specific font usage.

When Elizabeth's secretary, Joan, arrives, they sit down together and outline a plan of action.

⋯⋯⟩ Copy the memo onto official letterhead and deliver it to everyone in the company. Fax it to the remote sales offices.

⋯⋯⟩ Cancel all of Elizabeth's appointments and call the executive staff together for an emergency meeting.

⋯⋯⟩ Contact the two VPs in Seattle and have them fly back immediately.

When Joan leaves Elizabeth's office she makes the required phone calls, retrieves the memo from the printer,
proofs it, and returns it to Elizabeth. They make the final
corrections, print it again, and Joan literally runs to the
copier room.

Joan begins to make 400 copies, one for every employee,
and a couple of dozen extra to have on hand. But every
20 pages or so the copier jams. She soon discovers there is
a set routine to opening and closing access doors in order
for the copier to work. At the 200th copy the machine
completely jams. Joan attempts to fix it, then phones
another employee for help. Together they get the copier
running and fifteen minutes later she has her copies.

**Murphy's Law of Office
Automation: The more
mechanical devices needed
to accomplish something,
the greater the odds one
of those mechanical devices
will not work.**

Joan faxes copies to the remote sales offices hoping the
graphs won't look too muddy. Then she enlists the help of
two other secretaries and together they divide CubeWorks
into equal distribution areas and begin to hand-deliver it.

An hour later Joan slides into the executive meeting only
to discover they are taking a break. "Joan," says Elizabeth
as the group starts filtering out of the boardroom, "please
make copies of those documents on the table and find
a way to get them to the VPs in Seattle. Looks like you'll
have to fax them."

**Three secretaries will spend
a good part of their morning
delivering a memo that could
have been delivered in seconds
using Adobe Acrobat software.**

Faxing a hundred pages will take longer than it will for
them to fly back, Joan wants to say, but Elizabeth is already
gone.

By 1995, 27 million computer users will have access to E-mail.

THE SIMPLE MEMO

Employee productivity can quickly become a slave to the paper document and the way information is communicated.

Businesses today have marvelous and powerful personal computers to create thousands upon thousands of documents; these same computers, however, are seldom used to process and distribute those documents to each other. Instead, documents are still hand delivered in one way or another – a method of distribution employed for centuries. Even faxing, a great technical stride in itself, delivers static pieces of paper which are then copied and hand-delivered. Express mail merely increases the speed of the hand delivery method. The photocopying machine increases the number of hands, sometimes exponentially.

While CubeWorks may be experiencing an atypical business day, the frantic pace should be recognizable to just about anyone. Using Adobe Acrobat technology, things could be different.

Elizabeth composes her two-page memo using the Cube-Works corporate typeface and the graphs that depict the current financial status of the company. Instead of printing a master to be photocopied, Elizabeth uses Adobe™ Acrobat™ software to print it electronically. The new electronic document is an exact copy of the original, containing everything the hard copy has, including formatting, fonts, graphics, and its official look.

Adobe Acrobat technology allows documents to be distributed to a variety of personal computers and workstations while maintaining the integrity of the original.

She "attaches" the electronic document to a standard E-mail message for all employees. The file becomes an "enclosure" with the E-mail message, and employees receive the official memo almost instantaneously. No hand delivery. Each employee "views" the memo exactly the way Elizabeth created it, even those transmitted via modem to the remote sales offices.

Each employee has the same options: they can either read it on the screen or print it out. It can also be stored in their computers for later viewing or printing.

Using Adobe Acrobat software is easier than one might think. Since it is a document communications tool, not a creation application, it makes no difference what application is used to create a document – almost any application will work with Acrobat software.

The recipient of such a file does not need the same computer platform as the creator. A Macintosh-created document can be viewed easily on a PC running under Windows, and vice-versa. Neither does the recipient need the same application used to create the document, nor the actual fonts used in the document, to view or print it. Adobe Acrobat technology allows true cross-platform, device-independent viewing and printing of documents.

Without Adobe Acrobat technology, CubeWorks is a study in lost productivity. Elizabeth and her co-workers will run in circles communicating the numbers, facts, and information needed to guarantee that they win over The Zeb Group. When Elizabeth thinks over the corporate downsizing CubeWorks has already done, it's amazing how much lost productivity and needless money is spent communicating and processing documents.

The simple two-page memo is just the beginning of what Adobe Acrobat technology can really accomplish.

Documents no longer have to follow the traditional method of creation, printing, copying, and hand delivery. Adobe Acrobat software makes the process as short as creation and electronic distribution.

You do not have to reinvest in new applications or new systems or new networks or new fonts to make Adobe Acrobat software work for you.

page 121 Adobe Acrobat software writes and reads (views) to a file format called the Portable Document Format or PDF. "Portable" in this case means "mobile" or able to be ported to different computer operating systems. The Portable Document Format is based on the PostScript programming language, also from Adobe Systems.

You will see "PDF" frequently in this book and there will also be references to the PostScript language. Both refer to a level of computer science not covered here, but it's useful to know that PDF and PostScript are not the same thing. PDF is a file format used by the Adobe Acrobat family of products to describe the structure of an electronic document.

Of the Acrobat products discussed in this book, two actually "create" PDF files: Acrobat PDF Writer and the Acrobat Distiller *pages 69-71* program. Acrobat Exchange and Acrobat Reader are the applications for viewing the files created by the above programs. The PDF Writer is installed into your computer system when Acrobat Exchange is installed. Acrobat Distiller is a separate program.

A printer driver interprets information from the computer into a language a printer understands. The PDF Writer does the same thing but translates the information into an electronic PDF file.

PDF Writer

Acrobat PDF Writer is a printer driver, similar to other printer drivers used to print documents, except the PDF Writer "prints" an electronic file (in Portable Document Format). The PDF Writer is not an application, but part of the computer system. The PDF Writer printer driver is platform specific: when you install Acrobat Exchange for Windows, a PDF Writer for Windows is automatically installed onto your computer, and likewise for the Macintosh.

Acrobat Exchange

Acrobat Exchange has a number of tools and features that allow viewing, annotating, copying, printing, and general maneuvering through electronic documents. Acrobat Exchange "views" PDF files that have been electronically "printed" using the PDF Writer or the Acrobat Distiller program. Acrobat Exchange is also platform specific; the Macintosh version of Acrobat Exchange should be installed onto a Macintosh computer.

Acrobat Exchange and Acrobat Reader are the "viewing" applications. PDF Writer and Acrobat Distiller are the PDF creating programs.

Application   PDF Writer   Acrobat Exchange

Acrobat Distiller

The Acrobat Distiller program creates PDF files from PostScript language files. It is meant for electronic documents that are complex or contain a varied use of illustrations, photos, and other graphics, or for documents created with page-makeup programs such as QuarkXPress, PageMaker, FrameMaker, and many others. Acrobat Distiller is explained in greater detail later in this book.

 pages 78-81

PostScript Language File   Acrobat Distiller   Acrobat Exchange

Remember: Only PDF files can be viewed in Acrobat Exchange. Regular application files must be converted into PDF files.

Using the PDF Writer

Using the PDF Writer is as easy as printing a document to a printer. Once Acrobat Exchange is installed, almost any software application can create PDF files using the PDF Writer. If all employees in any given business have Acrobat Exchange on their systems, then everyone can publish, view, and share documents in PDF format.

To publish any simple document, print the document through the PDF Writer, rather than using the usual printing procedures:

·····⟩ Select the "Print" procedure for your computer system as outlined in the Acrobat Exchange documentation.

·····⟩ A print dialog box appears.

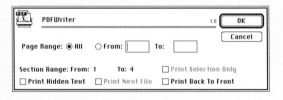

·····⟩ Enter the pages for which you want to create a PDF file.

The result is a slightly compressed electronic PDF file. Just like regular printing, nothing happens to your original file – it remains intact on your computer.

Keep the ".pdf" suffix in place because it identifies the file in cross-platform and electronic mail transfer.

PDF files are saved with the suffix ".pdf" so that a file named "CWmemo" will be saved as "CWmemo.pdf." This electronic file can be sent or accessed like any other electronic file via local network, or sent over phone lines via modem.

It's that simple. Create a PDF file, then share, view, and print on demand. The obstacles to printing, sharing, and viewing among diverse computer users become irrelevant.

Creating Annotation Notes

Printing, sharing, and viewing documents are the immediate benefits of Acrobat technology; information can retain the look, feel, format, and typography of the original. But what about that office mainstay, the "sticky" note, huge numbers of which get attached to paper documents?

One of the features Acrobat Exchange users will immediately grasp and begin to use is the Note Tool. With the Note Tool, electronic notes are created and attached to the electronic document. These electronic notes will ride along with the electronic document throughout the networks of the world.

To attach a note to a PDF file:

----> View any PDF file document.

----> Choose the Note Tool and select any area of the screen.

Note Tool

----> A window automatically appears and you can begin typing your note.

----> The note window can be made smaller or larger to accommodate the text.

This is the window for typing in annotation notes in Acrobat Exchange.

Fred, 6/16, 8:55am

Note Tool window

----> When the note is finished, close the window and it becomes a small note icon. On color monitors it appears as yellow. You can move the note anywhere on the page, and you can include as many notes in a document as you wish.

Note icon

Anyone at CubeWorks can not only open Elizabeth's memo and read it, but write several notes and attach them to it. They could be notes to other people, or notes to themselves, or notes that will stay with the document even a year or two from now. The glue is that good.

Every second 5,000 pounds of paper are used.

9:00 am

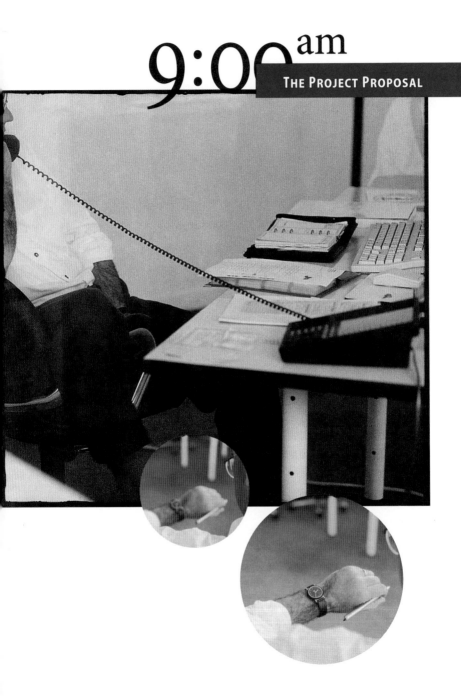

Jack Waegel is in charge of product marketing at Cube-Works. His current product responsibilities include a new design for contemporary partition walls; CubeWorks believes it can add enormous value to their product line by updating their older models to a more stylish design. Jack has just listened to a voice mail message from Elizabeth James: CubeWorks has a potentially huge new contract and an official memo will be forthcoming soon.

In the meantime, Jack must finish his project proposal for a meeting on Friday with all the major players of the product development team. This is the first meeting of the team with full representation from all four divisions of CubeWorks: Sales, Marketing, Manufacturing, and Engineering. As product marketing manager, Jack's responsibility is to complete the product on time while maintaining a balance between what the market wants and what engineering and manufacturing can accomplish. The delivery of timely information to Jack's peers and associates is critical.

Jack considers E-mail to distribute the project proposal but the contents are far too complex for electronic mail – there are several spreadsheets, tables, and illustrations. He also briefly considers sending out the electronic files but knows from experience that not everyone uses his application programs.

Jack will have to print, copy, and then send his document via interoffice mail to those attending the meeting. If he had the time he would hand deliver the project proposal himself.

This morning's priority is to create a project proposal. Once finished, Jack will distribute the document to the twenty-odd attendees so he can receive feedback before the meeting.

The marketing group uses Macintosh computers, the sales group uses PCs running on the Windows system, and the engineering and manufacturing groups run a combination of both plus UNIX.

When information is in transit between sender and receiver, it is called information float. Most paper documents have very long periods of information float.

Documents created on personal computers often use more than one software program – sharing them means each recipient needs the same software programs, not to mention the same operating system and computer platform – or you can print, copy, and use interoffice mail.

Jack created most of the pieces of his document over the past two months, and some sales data over the past year. While he waits for more on Elizabeth James' announcement, he pulls the project proposal together from various files on his computer. Pieced together are all the action items, the different divisions' to-do lists, an elaborate Gantt schedule table from the present to product-ship date, and the actual product specification.

Each piece of the project proposal is created using different software. For one-third of his proposal he uses a word processing application, for another third it is a spreadsheet, and for the final third Jack uses project tracking software.

As Jack completes each segment, he prints a copy from that application, and then moves onto the next segment. While he is keying in corrections, Joan stops by and delivers an official-looking memo from Elizabeth James. The more he reads the more excited Jack becomes. The Zeb Group contract and his product ship date look like they might coincide! He likes Elizabeth's phrasing in the memo so well that he types two complete paragraphs from it into his introduction to the project proposal.

When the master copy is complete Jack walks to the copier room, completes his twenty copies, and returns to his office and stuffs the documents into interoffice mail envelopes, writing each recipient's name on the envelope after looking up their building and office location from the master phone list.

The dotted line is not a graph. It represents the convoluted path of the mail cart that delivers interoffice mail.

A quick glance at his watch and Jack is alarmed at the additional hour that has just passed. But he's done. A productive morning's work is complete and the proposal is finalized. He is re-reading Elizabeth's memo when the mail boy stops by and picks up the twenty interoffice envelopes.

The mail boy listens to Jack's instructions on the importance of the interoffice envelope contents and the speed in which they should be delivered. "Is there any way you can deliver these first?" Jack asks. The mail boy looks listlessly at the mail cart which is very, very full of packages and envelopes. "I'm not feeling very well, Mr. Waegel, but I'll certainly try to get these out before quitting time."

Paper documents ultimately have to be delivered. The more recipients, the more complex the delivery path, and the longer the information float.

After the mail cart rumbles down the hallway, Jack decides to leave voice mail for all twenty recipients of his proposal. Jack reminds them about the Friday meeting and says a complete project proposal is in interoffice mail. Please check your mail tomorrow morning and if you haven't received it, Jack says, I'll deliver one myself.

One out of every five paper documents is filed away in file cabinets. The remainder are discarded.

Keeping people informed about new developments is crucial. If the information about Jack's project does not move quickly enough, or does not reach the right people at the right time, a serious gap can occur between Elizabeth James and her executive staff and Jack Waegel and his development team.

The stylish details and value-added features of the new cubicle partitions might help convince The Zeb Group to select CubeWorks as their primary vendor.

Jack is correct in assuming E-mail is not an effective vehicle for his project proposal document. His document has tables and graphics that are too complex for E-mail, and at about fifteen pages, much too long for that electronic delivery system. Jack is also correct in assuming that many recipients do not have his applications programs, the fonts he uses, or a computer operating system similar to his own. His only choice before Adobe Acrobat software was to copy, mail, and wait.

Using Adobe Acrobat software Jack can create a master PDF file of his project proposal and deliver it to his distribution list within seconds.

Instead of printing multiple copies and using interoffice mail, Jack uses the Acrobat software to create an electronic PDF document that everyone on his list can view, and then print if they care to do so. Jack sends his document attached to an E-mail message, or posts it on the network server. He then voice mails or E-mails the recipients about its network location and the necessity of getting their responses back to him.

A single PDF file can be read by Macintosh, Windows, DOS, and UNIX platforms. You don't have to create four separate documents.

Jack's PDF document can be read by all CubeWorks' employees who have an Adobe Acrobat viewing application installed on their workstations. A recipient using a Macintosh can see the document created by Jack; a recipient on a PC can see the document created by Jack; recipients using DOS and UNIX systems can also see Jack's document. All four computer platforms will view the PDF document in the exact same way.

Adobe Acrobat technology allows documents to be "portable" and to be device-independent, but once a PDF document is received a whole new set of features and benefits is enabled.

page 121

Suppose Martha can't make Jack's meeting, even though she is a critical member of the project team. When Martha receives the PDF document, and reads it, she can attach her comments to the PDF document, save it, and then forward the annotated file to her associate, Kiyotaka, who can attend the meeting. If Kiyotaka couldn't attend the meeting, Kiyotaka could add additional comments to the document while still retaining Martha's original notes, and pass it on to another associate. PDF files can be forwarded and passed along to other recipients ad infinitum, with changes intact.

PDF documents also stand the test of time: documents that are electronically archived will retain any and all alterations. A year or two from now, Martha's comments will still be embedded into Jack's original PDF document. One of the best features of PDF documents allows Martha to add her comments and send it back to Jack along the same electronic route. Information float in this instance, is negligible.

Remember when Jack copied the two paragraphs from Elizabeth's memo to his own document? Why manually key text? Acrobat technology supports copying text from PDF files to other application or system files.

Adobe Acrobat software gives PDF documents a robustness and intelligence that paper documents lack. The ability to search for specific words, annotate, copy and paste, and even add hypertext links (a feature discussed further on), are just a few of the features of Adobe Acrobat software. The ability to deliver documents to cross-platform computer environments (or even homogenous computer environments) in a timely manner is what many business people call a competitive edge.

The dotted line is the electronic path of a PDF document: it goes directly from sender to receiver.

Acrobat Exchange has several features for viewing, maneuvering, and searching through documents. The following eight pages show Acrobat Exchange for Windows, Acrobat Exchange for Macintosh, Acrobat Exchange for DOS, and Acrobat Exchange for UNIX and how they appear on the computer screen.

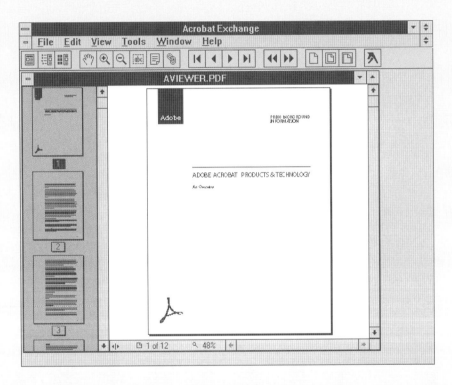

Screen Areas

Document Pane: This is the area for viewing documents.

Overview Pane: This area can be extended or collapsed. It allows either Bookmark or Thumbnail views.

Tool Bar: This area offers tools to view, manipulate, search, and annotate documents.

Viewing

 View Page Only: To view only the document pane.

 View Bookmarks and Page: To view both the document and Bookmarks together.

 View Thumbnails and Page: To view both the document and Thumbnails together. A scroll bar scrolls through the Thumbnails.

Navigation Tools

 Hand Tool: Use to move the page around in the active window.

 Zoom In Tool: Increases the magnification view at set increments.

 Zoom Out Tool: Decreases the magnification view.

 Select Tool: Select text for copying. The items can then be pasted into other applications, or a system clipboard.

 Note Tool: Create an annotation note anywhere on the page.

 Link Tool: Create an interactive link from one item to another item.

Page View

 Actual Size: View the document page at 100% size.

 Fit Page to Window: View the entire page by fitting it entirely into the document pane.

 Fit Width to Window: View the page by fitting the width of the page into the document pane.

Browse Tools

 First Page: Go to the very first page of the document.

 Previous Page: Go to the previous page.

 Next Page: Go to the next page.

 Last Page: Go to the very last page of the document.

 Go Back: Retrace your path through a document by going back.

 Go Forward: Retrace your path through a document by going forward.

Searching

 Search: Search for text.

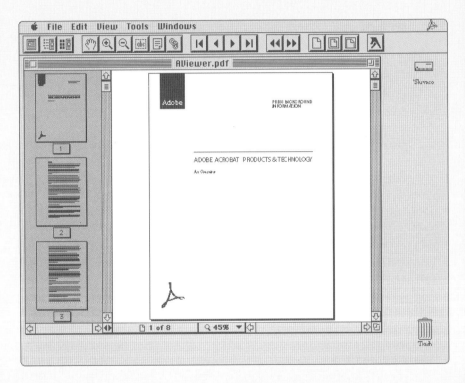

Screen Areas

Document Pane: This is the area for viewing documents.

Overview Pane: This area can be extended or collapsed. It allows either Bookmark or Thumbnail views.

Tool Bar: This area offers tools to view, manipulate, search, and annotate documents.

Viewing

 View Page Only: To view only the document pane.

 View Bookmarks and Page: To view both the document and Bookmarks together.

 View Thumbnails and Page: To view both the document and Thumbnails together. A scroll bar scrolls through the Thumbnails.

Navigation Tools

 Hand Tool: Use to move the page around in the active window.

 Zoom In Tool: Increases the magnification view at set increments.

 Zoom Out Tool: Decreases the magnification view.

 Select Tool: Select text for copying. The items can then be pasted into other applications, or a system clipboard.

 Note Tool: Create an annotation note anywhere on the page.

 Link Tool: Create an interactive link from one item to another item.

Page View

 Actual Size: View the document page at 100% size.

 Fit Page to Window: View the entire page by fitting it entirely into the document pane.

 Fit Width to Window: View the page by fitting the width of the page into the document pane.

Browse Tools

 First Page: Go to the very first page of the document.

 Previous Page: Go to the previous page.

 Next Page: Go to the next page.

 Last Page: Go to the very last page of the document.

 Go Back: Retrace your path through a document by going back.

 Go Forward: Retrace your path through a document by going forward.

Searching

 Search: Search for text.

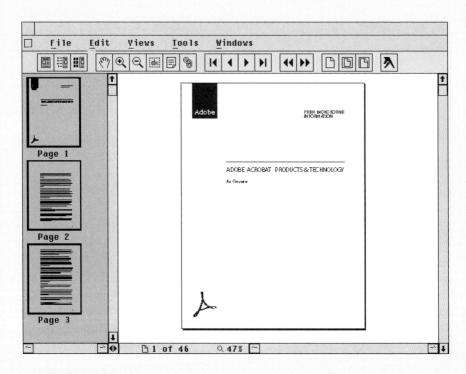

Screen Areas

Document Pane: This is the area for viewing documents.

Overview Pane: This area can be extended or collapsed. It allows either Bookmark or Thumbnail views.

Tool Bar: This area offers tools to view, manipulate, search, and annotate documents.

Viewing

 View Page Only: To view only the document pane.

 View Bookmarks and Page: To view both the document and Bookmarks together.

 View Thumbnails and Page: To view both the document and Thumbnails together. A scroll bar scrolls through the Thumbnails.

Navigation Tools

 Hand Tool: Use to move the page around in the active window.

 Zoom In Tool: Increases the magnification view at set increments.

 Zoom Out Tool: Decreases the magnification view.

 Select Tool: Select text for copying. The items can then be pasted into other applications, or a system clipboard.

 Note Tool: Create an annotation note anywhere on the page.

 Link Tool: Create an interactive link from one item to another item.

Page View

 Actual Size: View the document page at 100% size.

 Fit Page to Window: View the entire page by fitting it entirely into the document pane.

 Fit Width to Window: View the page by fitting the width of the page into the document pane.

Browse Tools

 First Page: Go to the very first page of the document.

 Previous Page: Go to the previous page.

 Next Page: Go to the next page.

 Last Page: Go to the very last page of the document.

 Go Back: Retrace your path through a document by going back.

 Go Forward: Retrace your path through a document by going forward.

Searching

 Search: Search for text.

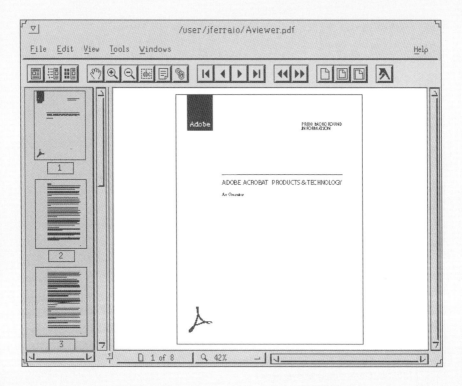

Screen Areas

Document Pane: This is the area for viewing documents.

Overview Pane: This area can be extended or collapsed. It allows either Bookmark or Thumbnail views.

Tool Bar: This area offers tools to view, manipulate, search, and annotate documents.

Viewing

 View Page Only: To view only the document pane.

 View Bookmarks and Page: To view both the document and Bookmarks together.

 View Thumbnails and Page: To view both the document and Thumbnails together. A scroll bar scrolls through the Thumbnails.

Navigation Tools

 Hand Tool: Use to move the page around in the active window.

 Zoom In Tool: Increases the magnification view at set increments.

 Zoom Out Tool: Decreases the magnification view.

 Select Tool: Select text for copying. The items can then be pasted into other applications, or a system clipboard.

 Note Tool: Create an annotation note anywhere on the page.

 Link Tool: Create an interactive link from one item to another item.

Page View

 Actual Size: View the document page at 100% size.

 Fit Page to Window: View the entire page by fitting it entirely into the document pane.

 Fit Width to Window: View the page by fitting the width of the page into the document pane.

Browse Tools

 First Page: Go to the very first page of the document.

 Previous Page: Go to the previous page.

 Next Page: Go to the next page.

 Last Page: Go to the very last page of the document.

 Go Back: Retrace your path through a document by going back.

 Go Forward: Retrace your path through a document by going forward.

Searching

 Search: Search for text.

*From 1982 to the year 2000,
projected world demand for paper and paperboard is expected
to almost double to 310 million metric tons.*

coffee break

Smart computer users rest their eyes from the flickering screen at set intervals. That's why Adobe Acrobat software gives users the option to print *or* view documents. The choice is yours, but we predict many documents will live their entire lives in electronic form, passed on from viewer to viewer. The savings in paper, and in time spent processing all that paper, is immense. But since this is a coffee break, let's talk about something else: staples.

Staples. Predictions of a stapleless office have circulated ever since the personal computer became popular. At an average cost of, let's say, $5 per stapler, a corporation with 100,000 employees could save, yes, $500,000. Better yet, the government, with millions of employees, could cut the size of the deficit by a modest amount (or at least be able to afford an extra space station toilet or two).

To suggest the potential cost savings of staples would be reaching too far, but the relief of not being pierced by stapled documents is reason enough to switch to electronic document communication.

Paper clips. The flimsy paper clip box always seems to disintegrate in your hands. A thousand paper clips scatter onto the carpet or floor with such vigor it seems they'd do anything to evade the box. The paper clamp, on the other hand, built for the 747 of documents, might go the way of the dinosaur. Made for wide-body documents, there are never enough in the box unless you buy the very, very small clamps where a paper clip would do just as nicely.

Time to take a break. Not all documents are all business, many in fact, are meant to entertain. The next coffee break, by the way, will be at 2:45 pm.

Some time in the near future, you'll show your age when mentioning that stalwart friend of the paper document, the paper clip.

And binders! Try to put five or more large binders together on a book shelf. Their triangular shapes just don't sit side-by-side very well. They weigh as much as a small notebook computer and the pages will never turn easily over the binder rings, no matter how hard you try.

Binders have spawned a whole subset of office products: the binder-hole punch that cuts binder-holes in the paper but never accepts more than five pages at a time; those little binder-hole strengtheners, a white vinylish concoction you are actually expected to lick and place over binder holes so the paper won't tear; and the all-time favorite, binder spine labels – after writing on the label you're supposed to slide it down the clear vinyl spine label protector without jamming the paper. Why does every country in the world seem to have a different standard for the number and placement of binder holes on paper?

File cabinets are great places to store all those paper documents if it wasn't for all the file cabinet paraphernalia. There are hanging file folders, manila folders, clear plastic label protectors, file folder labels, and file cabinet drawer labels. The cabinets themselves come in various sizes to accommodate normal, legal, and colossal size documents, so good luck jamming a 50-page legal-size document into a business-size document file cabinet (they go underneath all the hanging files).

Envelopes have their own uses and one cannot blame them for being slaves to the paper sealed inside. Envelopes give every letter its own gift wrapping. Unless, of course, it's a sweepstakes offer where the entire contents of the inside letter are printed on the outside of the envelope. Future mystery writers may have to invent another murder implement other than the letter opener.

Scissors are the most useful paper tool in the whole world. They will always have a prominent place in offices around the globe. Especially when you're looking for a screwdriver and you finally resort to using the end of a scissor blade to loosen a screw.

Interoffice envelopes may finally be laid to rest. Does anyone understand why there are holes in the envelope? Do paper documents need to breathe?

This does not signal the demise of office supply stores, but one's desk might be a little tidier for lack of all that paper paraphernalia. Adobe Acrobat technology allows both viewing and printing. You have the option – but no longer the obligation – to print, route, and copy more and more pieces of paper to such an extent that your trips to the supply room become more frequent than those lengthy trips to the copier room.

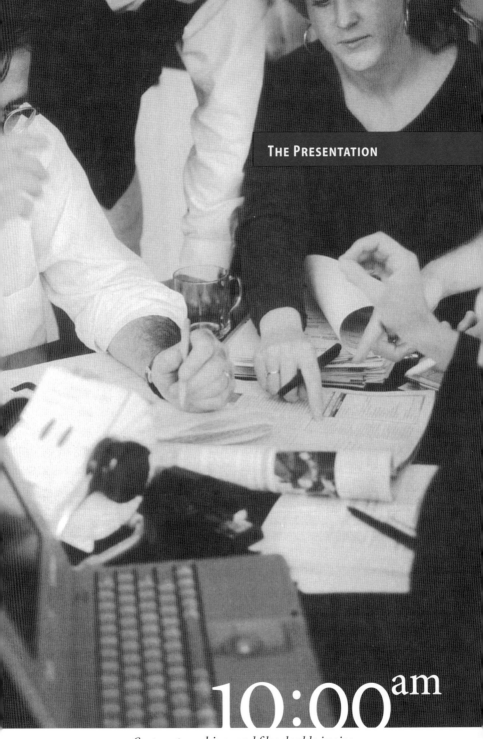

10:00^{am}

Corporate archives and files double in size
and in volume every 3.5 years.

Jackson Dunham, the Marketing Communications manager at CubeWorks, reports directly to Elizabeth James, even though he isn't a member of the executive staff. Jackson manages all marketing communication activities for CubeWorks and except for meetings like the emergency staff meeting that began at 10:00 am today, he is usually well informed and prepared for all of CubeWorks' marketing efforts.

When Jackson enters the executive staff meeting he is quickly briefed about The Zeb Group by Elizabeth James. Without pausing, she asks what marketing materials his department can pull together for a presentation to The Zeb Group; it should include the entire product line of CubeWorks (all 126 components), yet be adaptable to The Zeb Group interests.

Management 101 taught Jackson to respond to a question with a question: "Do we know what products they are interested in?" Elizabeth shakes her head. "We could make assumptions based on the information we have about the City Center complex, but no, Jackson, we don't know what products should or shouldn't be in the presentation. Be able to do them all." Okay, Jackson replies, but he wants to do the presenting, "I'll try to surmise what they want as I go along." Elizabeth agrees, then sits in silence. Jackson takes the hint and excuses himself. Just before Jackson exits Elizabeth says "I want to see what you have by 4 o'clock, Jackson."

48 | 49

Documents present information on the static medium of paper. Electronic documents can present information dynamically.

By the looks on the other faces in the conference room, everybody was getting their share of impossible deadlines.

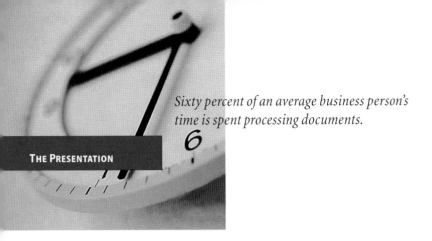

Sixty percent of an average business person's time is spent processing documents.

Most applications do not support each other. Here Jackson's staff has to manually change the data from a desktop publishing program to a presentation program. The format is changing but not the information.

When Jackson meets with his four-member staff he explains what happened at the meeting and then discusses the importance of The Zeb Group's contract. After toeing the company line for a few minutes, he begins the good news – bad news proposition. The good news is that we can play a major role in selling this huge contract to The Zeb Group, Jackson tells them, and the bad news is that we need to create and complete the presentation by Friday for an executive review. Then, before they can react, Jackson tells them Elizabeth wants to see what they can come up with by 4 pm.

To his surprise his staff reacts calmly. Shock, he tells himself, but they come up with a plan quite quickly. Since the group has already created all their data sheets with desktop publishing software, they have the text and the digital photos on hand. They will simply take what they already have and move it to a presentation application. The presentation will be computer generated and Jackson can use the projection system in the boardroom. There he will be able to adapt his presentation to The Zeb Group's interests by clicking on the mouse. After taking a few minutes to decide who will do what, the four-member group begins to work on the presentation.

····⟩ One staff member creates a template in the presentation software application.

····⟩ A second goes into every electronic data sheet and extracts the text files.

····⟩ A third member goes into every electronic data sheet and cuts and pastes the photos into separate files.

····⟩ The fourth prepares an outline and storyboard of the presentation, dividing the 126 products into four distinct families.

After a few intense hours, they take a break, and coordinate the next procedure. All the information has been digitally extracted from the desktop publishing software. All they have to do now is paste the particulars into the presentation application's template, beginning with a copy of the master presentation template. They each choose one of the four product families, and then paste in the contents of the data sheets.

By the end of tomorrow the template will be edited and fine tuned. Two days are needed to re-format existing digital information.

By 4 o'clock they are almost finished with the first pass of the presentation. There is so much data that it has to be separated into four presentation files; this will put some strain on Jackson during the actual meeting because he will have to quit one file before he can access another.

They encounter one other problem: which paper handout do they give to The Zeb Group? The actual data sheets, which are already handsomely printed, or copies of the presentation template? The information is identical but The Zeb Group will have gone through the presentation template, not the actual data sheets. They decide to give away both packages of information, so one staff member goes off to start preparing the paper handouts.

**4 staff members for 2 days
= 66 hours @ $25.00 per hour
= $1650.00**

By the year 2000 over 75% of the world's office workers will have access to a personal computer.

The projection system in the boardroom at CubeWorks displays what the PC screen shows, only much larger. It is here that The Zeb Group will watch Jackson maneuver through his presentation. The impromptu questions that arise about this product or that will be supported by the presentation.

Most people think of viewing documents on a personal level: one person creates a document in front of the computer screen, then another views it. However, if the screen is large enough, an entire audience can "view" the electronic document.

While Jackson's staff is certainly hardworking, had they used Adobe Acrobat software, a lot of work, time, and money could have been saved. The presentation could have been a study of simplicity.

Jackson's staff already created all their data sheets with their desktop computers, and each data sheet has all the needed information, including photos and specifications. Jackson's staff members now go to their original data sheet files, and create PDF files for each, eliminating the need to cut, paste, and copy information from one application to another (in this case a page-makeup application to a presentation application). The individual PDF data sheet files are then grouped into one master PDF file. In less than 2 hours an electronic document suitable for presentation on a projection screen to a large audience is finished.

Using Acrobat Exchange will empower any software application to create presentations. More importantly, different software can be used to create different pages within the same presentation, like spreadsheets, page makeup, or even calendar programs.

Remember the issue about handouts? The Acrobat presentation pages are exact renditions of the actual printed data sheets, complete with color, layout, and fonts. What The Zeb Group sees would be exactly what they get.

To give Jackson physical control over the presentation, his staff creates navigational controls that are built into the PDF document. In Acrobat Exchange there is an area of the screen where the user controls an "Overview Pane." This pane shows either Thumbnails of the pages in the document or Bookmarks. Selecting either of these overview items advances the document to "that" page. By creating Bookmarks and Thumbnails of the PDF presentation in Acrobat Exchange, Jackson's group gives Jackson the ability to maneuver all 126 products by a simple mouse or cursor movement. The presentation becomes much more intuitive and responsive to the needs of the audience, or of the moment.

page 36-43

The ability to navigate and maneuver through an electronic document is useful when building any electronic document – whether books, newsletters, documentation, or even presentations.

Another feature of Acrobat Exchange is its "Link Tool." With it a user creates "link buttons" from one part of a document to another. For instance, on a table of contents page, an invisible button could be created around the words Adjustable Desktop Product Data Sheet, and once saved, a simple mouse click on those words instantly takes the user to the exact data sheet.

Link Tool.

As soon as one becomes adjusted to the idea of electronic documents, then new possibilities begin to reveal themselves. Turn the page for a few fresh ideas…

4 staff members for 2 hours
= 8 hours @ $25.00 per hour
= $200.00

Navigating and maneuvering through a PDF document using Acrobat software is easier than with most presentation applications, especially with the navigational tools on the next four pages. But first some advantages of using Acrobat as a presentation platform.

⸱⸱⸱⸱⸱▹ Most presentation applications cannot open rival application files. With Acrobat technology it makes no difference whether it's Microsoft PowerPoint or Aldus Persuasion, or any of the other popular presentation software. Sharing the presentation across hardware platforms is effortless; Windows presentations can now be shared and actually "presented" on Macintosh computers.

How many times have you purchased software because you needed to "view" company presentations, not because you needed to create presentations?

⸱⸱⸱⸱⸱▹ Distributing PDF file presentations is done without worry of how the recipient is going to "open" it. Sales reps can give presentations to their clients or send them electronically. Notes can be attached by the recipients to annotate or explain items to their peers and management.

⸱⸱⸱⸱⸱▹ Acrobat software presentations are created from current software by creating PDF files. Unique presentations can be created from many different applications, not just presentation applications.

pages 102-105 ⸱⸱⸱⸱⸱▹ Interactive links can be created easily, by both the creator and the receiver.

Creating Thumbnails

The Overview Pane is the area of the Acrobat Exchange screen that contains Thumbnails or Bookmarks. These overview modes indicate not only where you are in the electronic document, but also where you might want to go. Thumbnails or Bookmarks can be inserted into any PDF file received or created, and the procedure is, again, quite easy.

⋯⋯▷ To create Thumbnails, choose the Create Thumbnails item from the Edit menu bar.

Creating Thumbnail sketches increases the size of a PDF file, which is one reason to delete Thumbnails if they are not needed or to send files without Thumbnails already included.

⋯⋯▷ A dialog box appears showing the status of the Thumbnails as each is created.

Clicking on any Thumbnail will take you to that page. In addition, a rectangular dotted line appears in the current Thumbnail page, representing the current area of the page that is visible on your computer monitor. Moving the dotted rectangle within the Thumbnail will move the page on the screen.

Creating Bookmarks

The Bookmark mode looks similar to a standard outline, except
selecting a Bookmark advances to the corresponding page and
view magnification. To create Bookmarks:

····⟩ Go to the page that requires a Bookmark. Select the viewing
magnification. (For example, "zoom" in on a picture, a word,
or a graph.)

····⟩ Choose Bookmarks, then New, under the Edit menu.

····⟩ A new untitled Bookmark is created. Select the "untitled"
Bookmark and type in the name you wish to give it.

····⟩ To delete a Bookmark, select a Bookmark, then choose
Delete Bookmark from the Edit menu.

Bookmarks can be arranged hierarchically, and any Bookmark
can be further delineated. Thus a Chapter 8 Bookmark can contain
dozens of other hierarchically arranged BookMarks (see below).

····⟩ Bookmarks can be moved, once created, by selecting any
Bookmark and actually moving it up, or down, or to the left
or right. Documents can have an altogether different Bookmark organization than the layout of their pages.

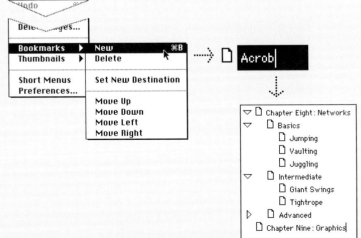

Navigating

Other navigational features can help you maneuver through an PDF document, whether its a six-page memo or a presentation.

In the View menu, and the corresponding tool bar at the top of the Acrobat Exchange window, are a series of Page Forward and Page Back buttons.

The Go Forward, Go Back buttons will retrace or advance the sequence of previous viewing by selecting the appropriate button. It is similar to finding your place in a book, except that you can retrace or advance along an entire path.

The vertical scroll bar will scroll through an entire document to find a specific page. The corresponding page numbers will change as the scroll thumb is moved down or up.

The Hand Tool allows the user to move a page that is being viewed in any direction. The magnification tools magnify or de-magnify the current view.

To maximize the viewing area, hide the tool bar and the Overview Pane – increasing both the height and width of the monitor space available for viewing.

These are just a few ways of navigating and maneuvering while viewing a PDF document within Acrobat Exchange. The interactive nature of Acrobat Exchange's tools is something that just can't be done on paper, and even in many software programs.

Every day 252 million original documents are created.

THE DIVERSE DOCUMENT

11:00^{am}

John Zeb started his mutual fund investment company not in a garage but in a converted auto repair shop.

That was twenty years ago, and now he is preparing to consolidate his company of 3,000 employees into the new City Center office complex. When it was decided to lease the City Center complex, John turned to Stacey Sacks to draw up a comprehensive plan for the move. Stacey's attention to details and her ability to coordinate complex projects makes her the ideal choice.

Many documents are comprised of bits and pieces of previously published and printed pages. With Adobe Acrobat software a PDF document can easily be created from the sum of its parts.

Compiling the various documents is a staggering prospect. There are executive briefing papers, internal specifications lists from the MIS department, numerous government and city code forms and white papers, comprehensive lists for purchasing, and, of course, the ever-changing schedule and status reports. Stacey's filing cabinets are crammed and her assistant, Mark, spends a good part of his time filing and re-filing the long and complicated paper trail.

When John Zeb calls Stacey at 11:00 am she is preparing for a meeting at 1:00 pm. John needs a complete move schedule, a requirements list for office cubicles and furniture, sample purchasing guidelines, and contracts. Further, Zeb wants numbers for the other office furniture suppliers they have worked with over the past year, and he would like this compilation for a meeting this afternoon.

An exasperated Stacey tells him it will mean missing a critical meeting. Sorry, John tells her. His meeting is with the mayor and he would like to hint at the prospect of buying office furnishings from a local manufacturer. It would greatly improve The Zeb Group's stature in the eyes of the local government and might help his push for lower local taxes.

On the average, it costs $200
to recover one misfiled document from cold storage.

When every department uses a different computer system, the only machine that bridges the communication lines is the copier machine.

The problem showed itself hundreds of times in recent months. Customizing documents to fit John's requirements is a nightmare. A few pages from a word processing document, some from a spreadsheet program, and a few more from a project management application. Stacey uses all these programs, but piecing them together is all but impossible. She prints the pages one at a time from each application, then collates them at the copying machine to make a master copy.

Stacey depends on Finance for the spreadsheet numbers and Facilities for weekly updates. They each use different systems, so she never gets the information electronically. Instead, she receives weekly reports and makes copies of them for her weekly reports.

The worst documents are always the most diverse. Some pages are created from Stacey's computer. Other pages are copies of copies and are barely legible. Still other pages are business-size, and legal size, and smaller sizes such as marketing brochures or handouts. Building a diverse document from all of these creates a document that is hard to read and hard to copy.

A photocopy

60 | 61

This time, John Zeb also wants some obscure numbers from almost a year ago. They are buried somewhere in her filing cabinets. Stacey calls Mark and asks him to begin searching for the reports.

Stacey starts to put together the needed elements, beginning with the most recent reports from Finance. She writes a quick note in her word processing application, then customizes a project memo she had previously written. These she prints out. Then she begins to search through her files and pulls out all the other elements of John's request.

Mark returns an hour and a half later with a folder full of files and letters he dug out of the filing cabinets. Together they go through them until they find a memo and a one-page spreadsheet that applies to John's request.

They copy the document to make a "copier" master, then feed it into the machine to make the required number of copies. It is now 2:30 and Stacey races off to the 1:00 meeting, hoping it is still going on. Mark distributes the document to John Zeb and his direct reports, then spends what is left of the afternoon refiling the cabinets he had overturned in his search.

of a photocopy   *of a photocopy*   *of a photocopy*
does not a document make.

By 1996 the number of copiers in the US is projected to be 6.7 million, producing 765 billion copies.

Horizontal pages can be inserted between vertical orientation pages, and pages of varying sizes can be combined together to create a truly diverse document.

John Zeb is remarkable in many ways, from the profitable way he runs the investment group to the way he treats his employees. And Stacey knows that when John needs something, he truly needs it. Using Acrobat software allows Stacey to get the report to John in the fastest, most efficient way possible.

Once Stacey completes her word processing introduction, she prints a PDF file. With each of her other applications she performs the same easy task of creating a PDF file. Using Acrobat Exchange she "inserts" new pages of the other PDF files at the correct place into the document. Saving the document means saving the larger, combined files into one single PDF document.

The Finance and Facilities departments publish their weekly reports using Adobe Acrobat software, so Stacey accesses the reports electronically, and then views them on her computer, despite the incompatible nature of their computers; she copies and pastes the information instead of typing it in manually, or simply inserts the pages into the new PDF file.

A copy of a PDF file

Inserting and deleting pages are normal requirements of information processing, whether you work on paper or electronically, but working with electronic documents has benefits that extend from the past into the near future.

If Stacey had printed all of her important or "filable" documents in the past year to PDF files, Mark's job would be greatly speeded by an electronic search through a hard disk, server, or back-up floppies. By searching for a key word, Mark would be able to find the precise page and even the exact sentence where any word occurs; the search feature even finds text embedded in graphics.

A year from now, this same PDF document, which is comprised of bits and pieces of other documents, will still be accessible. It can be searched, and copied, or have specific pieces of information extracted. Or this document can become a small piece of a much larger and more diverse document, making each and every document The Zeb Group creates an investment in the future.

of a copy of a PDF file   *of a copy of a PDF file*   *of a copy of a PDF file is still the original PDF file.*

Inserting Pages

Just because you've created a PDF file, doesn't mean you can't change it, or adapt it, or alter it. Unlike paper documents, a PDF document is still a "live" digital document that can be manipulated in diverse and creative ways. In fact, new documents can be made from pieces (pages) of other PDF documents; Inserting Pages and Deleting Pages is a key feature for inventive Acrobat users.

The screen shots on the next four pages are from both Macintosh and Windows platforms. Acrobat software has a similar user interface no matter which platform is used.

pages 36-43

Inserting pages within a PDF file is quite simple:

·····⟩ Open any PDF file

·····⟩ Choose Insert from the File Menu

·····⟩ Select the file you want to Insert (the file must be a PDF file)

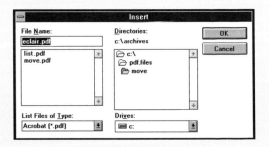

·····⟩ Choose where you want to insert the file (at the beginning, at the end, or between pages)

·····⟩ Save the file with a different name, for example *NewFile.pdf*.

If you receive a PDF memo from someone, you can insert another PDF memo into it the same way you might paper clip two paper documents together. Windows spreadsheet pages can be inserted into DOS database pages, which can then be inserted into Macintosh calendar/scheduling pages, which can then be inserted back into Windows word processing pages. As long as each of these instances are PDF files, then PDF pages and documents can merge together, even if every one of the pages brought together were created using different fonts. And, the entire document can be printed on your local area printer, and then held together with a paper clip.

Deleting Pages

Creating a new PDF document from several other PDF files will most likely involve deleting pages. For example, if you need pages 17 and 18 of a 28-page document, first delete pages 19 through 28, and then delete pages 1 through 16. (Of course you could always insert the full 28-page document and then delete – just keep track of the page numbering scheme.)

⋯⋯⟩ Open any PDF file

⋯⋯⟩ Choose Delete Pages… from the Edit Menu

⋯⋯⟩ Enter the pages you want to delete

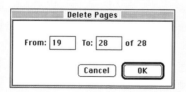

⋯⋯⟩ Save the document with a different name, for example, *NewFile.pdf.*

 page 81

Page Size and Orientation

Not every PDF file you want to insert into a new document will have the same page size or orientation. Most business memos have the standard US Letter (8 1/2- x 11-inch) size, but there is also US Legal, and the European standard A4 size. Marketing brochures vary in size, and books, such as this one, depend on a smaller, less unwieldy size for physical portability.

Creating diverse documents from pieces of other documents can be absolutely mind-boggling on the copier machine. Mass-producing a document that uses marketing brochure pages as well as normal business memos, means making copies of copies, or possessing an advanced degree in copier physics.

Page orientation is either vertical or horizontal, meaning the longer side of a rectangular piece of paper is either up and down, or left to right.

Acrobat Exchange easily addresses the dilemma of combining pages from documents that have a different page size and orientation because the documents are electronic. You do nothing different other than Insert Pages as described on pages 64 and 65; therefore, one page can be big, the next small.

Another feature is the Crop Pages command in the Edit menu. This allows you to physically "crop" or reduce the height or width of a page(s).

·····⊱ Choose the Crop Pages command from the Edit menu. A dialog box will appear. Simply input the amount that needs cropping into the measurement boxes (the amount is entered in points: 72 points equal 1 inch, 36 points equal a half-inch, and so on).

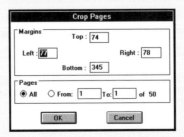

Rotating Pages

Acrobat Exchange is capable of inserting a horizontally oriented
page within a mostly vertical document. In fact, the orientation of
pages can be mixed and matched at will by choosing "Rotate Page"
from the Edit menu.

┈┈┈⟩ Choose the Rotate Page command from the Edit menu.

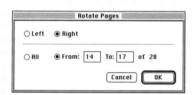

┈┈┈⟩ Enter the page range you wish to rotate and choose the
direction you wish to rotate: vertically (if already horizontal)
or horizontal (if already vertical).

These features of Acrobat Exchange create diverse documents that
vary in page size, orientation, and content. Together with some of
the navigation features already discussed on pages 54 through 57,
you can build dynamic documents from other documents that will
hold the attention of intended viewers. There's nothing like a little
color illustration or at least a small format variation to break the
monotony of an otherwise plain and straightforward document.

**When horizontal pages
are mixed with vertically
oriented documents, they
are called "broadsides."**

Each year 2 billion books,
350 million magazines,
and 24 billion newspapers are printed
in the United States.

ACROBAT READER AND ACROBAT EXCHANGE

lunch**break**

By this time of day you should be getting comfortable with the idea of creating and distributing electronic documents. Acrobat technology allows you to create, view, share, and print electronic documents in a variety of ways; there are also a number of ways documents can be distributed, from E-mail attachments, to accessible public folders, to directories on network-wide servers.

Fortunately, or unfortunately, depending on your lunching habits, this will be a business lunch. But don't worry, we'll do all the talking. Sit back and enjoy your pastrami and rye.

Large amounts of information can also be "published" on CD-ROMs. Imagine encyclopedias or large reference volumes consolidated onto a single CD. Entire libraries can be created as PDF files and included on CDs. Lawyers, doctors, and other professionals who rely on reference books will soon be able to view books as PDF files, with all the fonts, page make-up, and design characteristics embedded into the CDs.

With the interactive abilities of Adobe Acrobat technology, publishers can create amazing documents. An electronic magazine may not sound that exciting but think of the advertising possibilities. An advertisement for a car, for example, could have several layers of interactive links. Selecting the car on the computer screen might give the complete range of colors or models. Selecting another area could list the dealers in your area, or sweepstakes rules. Beneath each advertising page are layers and layers of additional information: your magazine suddenly has a 16-page marketing brochure embedded into every single page of the original.

▶ *page 117*

But before we go any further, it's time to discuss the two versions of the Acrobat viewing applications available as retail products; each has specific benefits and features. The first is Acrobat Reader, and the second is Acrobat Exchange.

Moving beyond paper will
take time and a familiarity
with the powers and
eloquence of document
interchange.

Acrobat Reader

Acrobat Reader is the view- and print-only version of
the Acrobat viewing applications. It is priced considerably
less than the full-feature Acrobat Exchange, and while
it offers the same viewing performance of Acrobat
Exchange, it has fewer capabilities.

Acrobat Reader can view any PDF file regardless of the
platform, system, or application that created the PDF file.
Acrobat Reader opens any size PDF file and PDF file
containing color. It also contains the complete font
substitution capabilities of Acrobat Exchange. Acrobat
Reader supports printing of the files it views: if it is a
PDF file then Acrobat Reader will print it.

Acrobat Reader does not have a "Save" function, so many
of the features of annotation notes, inserting and deleting
pages, or creating interactive links are not available. In
fact, Acrobat Reader comes with "short menus" so many
features discussed in this book are not visible. Once you
open a document in Acrobat Reader you can read and
print that document, or pass it on to someone else, but
changes cannot be made.

Many users of Acrobat technology will have no need to
modify electronic documents. For instance, in corporations that have a centralized publishing department,
some users need only be able to "receive" and "read"
documents. Other users might prefer the simpler viewing
mechanism before using the peer-to-peer communication
abilities of Acrobat Exchange. With Acrobat Reader,
users have a choice of Acrobat viewing engines that is best
suited to their working environment.

Acrobat Exchange

Acrobat Exchange is the premiere viewing application
for PDF files and documents. It has all the capabilities,
features, and benefits for peer-to-peer communication
across a network or around the world. When Acrobat
Exchange is installed onto your computer system, PDF
Writer is also installed, allowing the user to both create
PDF documents and to view them.

Acrobat Exchange is the fully functional application that
enables people and computers to communicate in unique
and novel ways. It supports viewing, printing, saving,
annotating notes, and all the other features and benefits
for document interchange and communications.

Acrobat Exchange and Acrobat Reader

The option of using either the read- and view-only
version, or the full-feature peer-to-peer application, will
empower people to experience the potential of Acrobat
technology at the level where they feel most comfortable.

Acrobat Reader provides the option to print *or* view documents. Acrobat Exchange offers capabilities and features
for maneuvering and manipulating document content
while communicating directly with users across all computer boundaries.

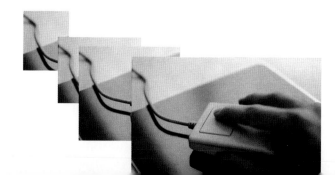

1:00^{pm}

New York City consumed
more than 750 million pounds of office paper in 1992.
Projected usage for 1995 is 800 million pounds.

If you're one of those people who take awhile to wake up, it's 1:00 pm and we have a confession to make about this morning. Some of the Acrobat product activity at CubeWorks, and at The Zeb Group, was not electronically "printed" using the PDF Writer, but by using Acrobat Distiller software. Our intention is to slowly move toward the point where you are comfortable creating and viewing electronic documents.

The PDF Writer is the simplest way to create a PDF file. As a printer driver, the PDF Writer works well for simple memos and text-only documents. Acrobat Distiller software, on the other hand is a full-fledged application that "distills" documents with PostScript graphics, heavy font usage, structured documents, and more. Many of the CubeWorks documents were distilled into PDF documents using Acrobat Distiller software.

It's very much like the difference between CubeWorks and our company for the rest of the day, Bythos Corporation. Bythos is a multi-conglomerate with offices around the globe. Their primary business is packaged foods. With over 15,000 employees, in 55 different buildings spread across 4 continents, Bythos has the financial backing that CubeWorks doesn't. What works for CubeWorks doesn't work for Bythos. And as we 'll soon discover, what works for Bythos often doesn't work for Bythos.

This afternoon we'll be joining the multinational Bythos Corporation for a few hours. Their document processing needs are much greater than CubeWorks and just as unique. Likewise, Adobe has an industrial-strength method of creating PDF documents – Acrobat Distiller.

Every business day 200 million pieces of paper are filed away in file cabinets.

THE INTERNAL DOCUMENT

Pierre Dupree is the Chief Operating Officer at Bythos, a French Canadian who is employee number two of Bythos. Employee number one is his partner, Fred Irwin, currently Chief Executive Officer. Pierre is the baker and Fred is the sales whiz. Together they began Bythos by selling graham crackers on the streets of Toronto.

Our appointment is with Anne Bennett, Vice-President of Human Resources, and Pierre. The agenda is about the new employee benefits program that will take effect in two months. The new employee benefits program is one of the most comprehensive in Bythos' history.

The goal for Bythos is to make the top ten list of the best corporations to work for in North America. The new benefits package might just allow them to compete for that honor.

Now some major decisions must be made on how to promote the program internally. Anne wants the marketing communications VP to develop an employee handbook, a flashy three-ring binder that can be updated as benefits change. The employee handbook will be massive but impressive-looking. There are almost 200 pages of health care benefits as well as corporate guidelines for hiring, employee leave, vacation and sick time, and pension and 401K programs.

Anne's plan, which she presents to Pierre, is to produce 20,000 handbooks and binders. Bythos should store about 5,000 extra in a warehouse for new hires and attrition replacement hires, or enough to last two years.

page 46 ◀ The estimated cost of the total employee handbook binder will be $30 each, or $600,000.

Distribution of the binders is estimated at $10,000, and updates on policies will cost $20,000 a year (including mailing). Anne feels that one new employee can mastermind the entire product, coordinating the writing, film, printing, binder assembly, mailing and distribution, and the many vendors involved in the film, printing, and binder assembly stages. That employee will cost $40,000.

Pierre sighs and stares out the window. Anne argues that the employee handbook could pay for itself in about two years: HR liaisons spend about 20 percent of their work week answering questions about health and other employee benefits. Pierre asks how much the forms for employee benefits cost. Anne estimates about $100,000.

Pierre finally agrees to the cost of the employee handbook. "No outside contractors or consultants. The cost of the benefits package itself is staggering without paying a fortune for the employee handbook." Then Pierre adds, "and find some way to get the cost down on all those damned forms."

Anne nods and ends the meeting commenting on how this program really will save time and money. "Every doughnut's got a hole," says Pierre, "and on this benefits thing it's definitely the handbook."

Paper processing costs…

	$600,000 printing
+	$10,000 distribution
+	$20,000 updating
+	$40,000 employee
=	$670,000

+	$100,000 forms
=	$770,000

Approximately 17 trees are cut down for every ton of paper made from virgin wood pulp.

THE INTERNAL DOCUMENT

While benefits are near and dear to employee's hearts, the employee handbook generally sits on employee's shelves. It is, at least, a reference document, read infrequently and only a section at a time. It is the perfect type of document to reside in electronic form on a network server.

The amount the information that flows through corporations is staggering. The ability to access that information whenever needed, in a timely, cost-efficient manner, is crucial to corporate effectiveness.

The process of electronically "creating" the benefits book in QuarkXPress, Aldus PageMaker, Microsoft Word, FrameMaker (or hundreds of other applications) is not affected by using Adobe Acrobat software. Color, design, photos, illustrations, formatting, and text fonts of the original are also unchanged by using Adobe Acrobat solutions for electronic documents. What does change – and dramatically at that – is the the cost of printing, processing, and distribution (not to mention film, printers, press checks, binding, and all those other production add-ons).

Updating these kinds of corporate documents means sending pages to employees for insertion in their binders. Everyone we know, except the most obsessive, puts the new pages in the front of the binder and forgets it, or they stuff the whole envelope into the binder, or put the envelope next to the binder on the shelf. Using the Acrobat

pages 64-65 ◄

Exchange insertion feature, new pages can be inserted and deleted easily and efficiently. Sending PDF files of updated pages over the Bythos network is also easy. Creating a new employee handbook and electronically distributing it would circumvent employees doing it all.

Once the marketing communications group has the finished pages of the employee handbook composed in their favorite application(s), they create a master PDF file and distribute it over the Bythos network. Employees can now download it from the server whenever they wish, or use the server to access those sections they want to review.

Employees can print the file or view it as an individual page, a single chapter, or the complete handbook. Imagine searching for "vacation policy" and actually finding the reference before you meet with your boss.

An important part of having the employee benefits handbook in electronic form is the savings to the corporation: film, printing, and binder assembly of the paper handbook are unnecessary. The distribution process is changed from sending out a 4-pound binder to accessing an 800K file from a Bythos server. Moreover, the printing and distribution of hard copy updates also becomes unnecessary.

Employees can have immediate access to the benefits forms as PDF files. They can download what forms they need, when they need them, and then either view or print the form.

Having this type of document on a company-wide server network accommodates the employee better than a paper copy because it allows instant access to the most current information, which in the long run is a tremendous employee benefit.

Electronic processing costs…

	$0 printing
+	**$1,000 distribution**
+	**$500 updating**
+	**$40,000 employee**
+	**$2,000 forms**
=	$43,500

·····⟩ Acrobat savings of
$726,500!

Acrobat Distiller software turns PostScript language files into PDF files, retaining all the powerful display and printing capabilities of the PostScript language.

Acrobat Distiller software transforms PostScript language files into documents in the Portable Document Format (PDF). It does not "view" PDF files, nor does it read them. As the name implies, it "distills" files from a programming language (the PostScript language) into a file format (PDF). The resulting files can then be viewed on any computer that has either the Acrobat Reader or Acrobat Exchange applications.

Acrobat Distiller software products

There are two versions of Acrobat Distiller software. One runs as a network application and is accessible to anyone with access to the network. The second version is a personal Acrobat Distiller program with the same power and features of the network program, but it runs on a personal computer or workstation providing that computer has adequate memory and disk storage.

When you must use Acrobat Distiller software...

Acrobat Exchange comes with a special-purpose printer driver called PDF Writer, which creates PDF files. There are some documents, however, for which the PDF Writer cannot create PDF files. For these documents, you must use an Acrobat Distiller program:

---> Documents created with high-end graphics programs and page layout programs. These programs use Encapsulated PostScript language (EPS) graphics.

---> Some applications (there are thousands of applications across computer platforms) may not allow the PDF Writer to write a PDF file.

┈┈⟫ Some computer platforms may not be immediately supported
with a PDF Writer (DOS, UNIX, OS/2, and other older system
software versions of Macintosh and Windows).

Benefits of Acrobat Distiller software

The benefits of having Acrobat Distiller software on your own
computer are immediate, however, Acrobat Distiller software will
be available to most users over a network. The benefits include:

┈┈⟫ You can use your computer to work on other jobs while
the network Acrobat Distiller creates your PDF documents.

┈┈⟫ A single network Acrobat Distiller program can support
hundreds of users.

┈┈⟫ Availability over a network means it can support anyone with
access to that network, even if that person is using a remote
access program in Chicago when Acrobat Distiller is physically
on a server in Miami.

┈┈⟫ Systems with small memories can still create PDF files
by accessing the network.

Acrobat Distiller software is a key component in creating PDF documents that can be ported to diverse computer platforms. Since
the Acrobat Distiller program "distills" PostScript language files
into PDF files, you need only create a PostScript language file from
your desktop application. The rest is accomplished by the Acrobat
Distiller application.

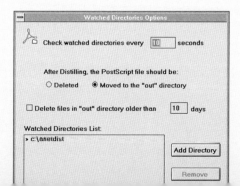

Creating a PostScript Language File

Acrobat Distiller software transforms PostScript language files into PDF files. First, create a PostScript language file from your application; like the PDF Writer, instead of printing the document to a local printer you will "print" an electronic PostScript language file.

Remember: **Acrobat Distiller will only distill PostScript language files. You cannot put your application file into the "In" folder or directory and expect anything to happen. Only PostScript files will be distilled.**

┄┄┄⟩ When you are satisfied with the content of your document, ask the application to print it, as if you were going to print to a local printer.

┄┄┄⟩ In the Print dialog box, select "PostScript File" instead of "Printer" as the document's destination.

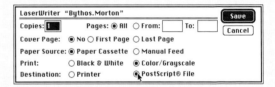

┄┄┄⟩ You will be asked to give the new PostScript file a name. We recommend you give that file a suffix of ".ps" to identify it as the PostScript copy of your original. So a file named *NewMemo* should be saved as *NewMemo.ps*.

┄┄┄⟩ The application writes the new PostScript file and saves it.

┄┄┄⟩ The PostScript file, *NewMemo.ps*, can now be processed by the Acrobat Distiller application, either on the network or resident on your computer.

Creating a PDF File
from a PostScript Language File

When Acrobat Distiller software is installed onto a network server or volume, it creates an "In" and an "Out" directory or folder. The network administrator does the installation and decides where the Acrobat Distiller will monitor these "In" and "Out" directories. The personal version of the Acrobat Distiller product works in the same manner:

To create a PDF file from your *NewMemo.ps* file:

⋯⋯⋚ Copy the NewMemo.ps into the "In" folder (or directory).

⋯⋯⋚ Continue working on your computer.

⋯⋯⋚ In a few minutes, access the "Out" folder (or directory). Your original *NewMemo.ps* file will be there along with the newly created *NewMemo.pdf* file. (The Acrobat Distiller program automatically adds the suffix ".pdf" to to all distilled files, but those ending with a ".ps" suffix will be replaced with a ".pdf" suffix.)

⋯⋯⋚ Copy the PDF file back to your computer. The "distilled" file is now compatible for viewing on Macintosh, Windows, DOS, or UNIX operating systems. Fonts, formatting, and graphics are exactly the same as the original document.

To keep track of the application, PostScript, and PDF versions of your documents, we again emphasize that you follow our suggested naming convention. So *NewMemo* becomes *NewMemo.ps* which then becomes *NewMemo.pdf*.

In

Out

2:00^{pm}

Morton Lee is head pastry chef at Bythos but he has a unique job classification: Pastry Chef/Writer. He doesn't write for popular cuisine magazines but instead develops recipes for all the pastries that Bythos makes. He is part of the Experimental Kitchens Group (EKG), which develops new packaged or frozen foods. Morton's recipes involve outrageously large portions: 20 barrels of vanilla, a truckload of sugar, 2,200 egg yolks, a big, big dash of nutmeg, and so on.

When Morton is not in his huge kitchen, he's writing detailed recipes for all the individual factories and bakeries, proposals for the marketing and promotions department, briefs for the executive staffs, compliances for the government regulators, features and benefits for the product marketers, nutritional databases for the customer service staff, and a memo or two to the other EKGs in all the other countries.

Devising recipes that taste good is difficult. Devising a recipe for a factory to produce 200,000 éclairs a night (that taste good) is even more difficult. Informing all the necessary Bythos people about the new fat-free, great-tasting éclairs is an adventure in communication that keeps Morton out of his beloved kitchen.

Morton's distribution list for new foods proposals includes over 200 people in North America, Europe, and Australia. Each proposal is about twenty pages long, sometimes thirty. Twenty to thirty pages to explain a maple-frosted, or dark-chocolate frosted custard éclair is normal. Add the fat-free part and all the fat that used to go into the pastry gets put into the product proposal.

In a corporation the size of Bythos, documents can quickly become quite complex because of the number of people who need to be informed. Until now, the method of delivering those documents in that kind of environment has simply been treated as the way things get done.

COMPLEX DOCUMENTS

The larger the organization the more dependent it is on relaying information between all its various departments.

Morton prepares the proposals and his assistants make thousands of copies; they fax a third of them, express mail another third, and send one-third of them through interoffice mail. He then waits several days for that hand-delivering, and walking, and jet planes, and faxing, and return hand-delivering, and return walking, and return faxing, and returning jet planes. Some of his proposals are so badly copied or faxed Morton can't read whether they say a barrel-full or a boat-full of heavy cream.

Morton does this about once every two weeks for the pastry EKG. The result, about 24 new or "improved" pastry proposals and recipes pass through Morton every year (only about a quarter ever make it to the consumers).

Bythos is a big corporation and they make more than just frozen pastries: frozen dinners, entrees, pizzas, a wide assortment of crackers and breads, condiments, packaged soups (dry and liquid), a gourmet line, and a fat-free line of instant camping foods. Just when a line of food stabilizes, customers change their eating habits, health habits, or vacation camping habits.

Bythos Research and Development depends on copying machines, express mail, normal mailing, illegible faxes, interoffice mail, lots of secretaries, and reams and reams and reams of recipes sent to literally thousands of people who have binders laying all over their desks, ovens, bookshelves, and kitchen floors. The archive department is probably the only organized area in the R&D group, but that's because it occupies its own building.

This is the way the world's corporations and businesses work. If it's not éclairs it's tires, or the entertainment industry, or finance, or appliances, or government. Information is relayed via documents, from legal contracts to spreadsheets. It's a fact. Look at your own job. You depend on a computer, a printer, a fax, a copier, express mail, and interoffice mail.

You will always use a copier, and a fax, and express mail, and interoffice mail even if you use Acrobat technology, because they are all useful tools. But now there is an alternative to buying an airplane seat to deliver an authentic-looking document somewhere, or faxing a poor facsimile to a fixed address.

Bythos has invested vast sums of money these past years updating the computer network and the personal computers of its employees. They already share information via E-mail, and file transfer, and remote access, and servers, gateways, and routers: the network is already there. If you use the computer to create a document why shouldn't you use the computer to distribute it? The savings to a corporation like Bythos would be astronomical: savings not only in dollars, but in the productivity of its employees and the accessibility to information.

Until that time, Morton will continue to spend up to 60 percent of his time coping with documents, not creating pastries.

If computers are used to create documents why shouldn't those very same computers be used to deliver, distribute, respond, and forward those documents?

◀ page 79

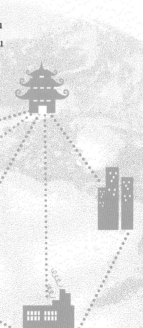

*The average office worker throws away about ½
pound of paper a day. An average worker in a financial institution wastes up to 2 pounds a day.*

QUIZ

Time for a quiz.

Use a number 2 pencil
to circle your answers.

Since you know that Morton is doing it all wrong, it's only
fair you help decide how he might do it right. Or at least
fast and inexpensively. Choose a method to help Morton
after each to-do task. Add up your score and discover
whether you're Acrobat-aware.

1. **After Morton finishes typing his fat-free éclair proposal
   he makes a master copy of it by:**
   a) Printing it to his local printer [$.25 / 5 minutes]
   b) Creating a PostScript language file and then creating
      a PDF file in an Acrobat Distiller program [$0 /5 minutes]

2. **To get the required 25 copies of the proposal, Morton:**
   a) Prints 25 more copies [$6.25 / 30 minutes]
   b) Makes 25 copies [$6.25 / 20 minutes]
   c) Copies the ECLAIR.PDF file from an Acrobat
      Distiller program to his personal computer [$0.00/min.]

3. **To send the 25 copies of the proposal, Morton:**
   a) Faxes 8 of them, express mails 7 of them, interoffice
      mails 8 of them [$80 / 1 hour]
   b) Sends E-mail to 25 recipients (some long distance,
      with the ECLAIR.PDF file as an enclosure)
      [$8.00/ 5min.]

4. **For Michael (Philadelphia) to get Morton's (San Francisco)
   proposal he must use:**
   a) A fax machine [$1.00 / 10 minutes for a bad facsimile]
   b) Express mail [$12.50 / 18 to 24 hours]
   c) Acrobat software [$1.00 / 10 minutes for a digital exact copy]
   d) Interoffice mail [not applicable]

5. When Morton (San Francisco) gets Michael's (Philadelphia) detailed response, Morton receives a copy from:

   a) A fax machine [$1.00 / a fax of a fax with writing upon it]
   b) Express mail [$12.50 / another 24 hours but legible]
   c) Acrobat software [$1.00 / Morton's original proposal with electronic notes attached]
   d) Interoffice mail [not applicable]

6. When the marketing department sends Morton a color photograph for the sample packaging, Morton receives:

   True or False? Four million dollars is more than four hundred thousand dollars?

   a) Faxed copy [$1.00 / 10 minutes for a solid black (no color) rectangle where the photo is supposed to be]
   b) Express mail [$12.50 / 18 to 24 hours]
   c) Acrobat software [$1.00 / 10 minutes for a full color image that Morton can annotate and send back]
   d) Description over the phone [$2.00 / not applicable – never trust phone descriptions of marketing work]

7. Now, the million-dollar question… Bythos employs over 15,000 people. Thousands of complex documents in a complex environment. Using question number 3 [$88.00/1 hour vs. $8/5 minutes], choose which makes better sense:

   a) There are 50 of these documents produced each day (1 per every 300 employees) for 340 days a year [$1,360,000/17,000 hours] vs. Acrobat [$136,000/1,416 hours]
   b) If there are 100 of these documents produced each day (1 per every 150 employees) for 340 days a year [$2,720,000/34,000 hours] vs. Acrobat [$272,000/ 2,832 hours]
   c) If there are 150 of these document produced each day (1 per every 100 employees) for 340 days a year [$4,080,000/51,000 hours] vs. Acrobat [$408,000/ 4,248 hours]
   d) Any of the Acrobat alternatives

Of course, the right answers are easy:
1b, 2c, 3b, 4c, 5c, 6c, 7d.
If you are not Acrobat aware, please
return to page 1.

You don't need to know much about type or fonts to work with Adobe Acrobat software, but it might help to understand the basics.

It's time to talk about fonts and how Adobe Acrobat technology solves the "font problem." Adobe knows quite a bit about type: it has one of the most complete cross-platform digital type libraries in existence, and it developed the remarkable multiple master font technology which is used by Adobe Acrobat software.

If you have ever received an electronic document from someone and you didn't have the font, then you know that your computer will automatically revert all text information to a default font. The look, feel, line breaks, italics, boldface, and hyphenation of the file you received will be completely askew. The document, in almost all cases, is unreadable and unmanageable.

The only way around this problem has been:

⋯⋙ Send the font with the document (but the memory size of the fonts used in a document is often larger than the document size itself).

⋯⋙ Keep documents in a font that you hope other people have (a guessing game)

⋯⋙ Just send a paper copy

When you install Acrobat Exchange (or Acrobat Reader) software onto your computer, the program will automatically install a special version of an Adobe product called ATM (Adobe Type Manager) into the computer system. It also installs two multiple master fonts into your system, Adobe Serif and Adobe Sans. These two multiple master fonts have the ability to emulate almost any font you might use in your document. When you create a PDF file (by using either the PDF Writer or Acrobat Distiller software), information about the font(s) that you use is included in that PDF file. When someone else opens your PDF file, Acrobat technology will substitute the Adobe Serif or the Adobe Sans typefaces (or both) for the original typefaces that you used.

Multiple master typefaces can do this because they offer an unlimited palette of font variations as well as the ability to generate custom fonts on the fly. They do this by using a design matrix based on one or more variables: weight, width, size, and style. This multidimensional approach to fonts enables Adobe Acrobat software to maintain the look and feel of documents not only across computer platforms, and software platforms, but also across (in lieu of a better word) font platforms. You are no longer restricted to a particular font for other people to view your document.

Acrobat font technology becomes especially important when sending documents between computer platforms because no two computer systems handle fonts quite the same way. Acrobat software will continue to substitute the multiple master typefaces and create near identical copies of the original typefaces no matter the platform. Acrobat software can do this because it's the PDF file that has the font information enclosed, not the computer system.

Adobe Acrobat will work with Type 1 or TrueType fonts. If you decide to print an Acrobat document from Acrobat Exchange or Acrobat Reader, the document will be able to print on both PostScript or non-PostScript laser printers, ink jet printers, or dot matrix printers.

While type substitution will be apparent to the trained typographer or experienced designer's eye, the vast majority of readers will never know. Turn the page and test your typographic eyes on a before and after example of Adobe Acrobat's font substitution technology.

The page below was printed in Quark XPress using Univers and ITC Century.

The Experimental Kitchens Group

The following proposal is for a new line of fat-free frozen élairs (Exquisite Éclairs) to be marketed under the Nature's Gourmet product line. Research has shown that fat-free gourmet pastries will have a solid impact on the market place given today's health conscious consumer.

Our éclair recipes have been carefully researched to use existing stock ingredients, substituting butter with oil and using our own egg substitute. This should reduce the caloric content of the éclairs by 35% and the fat content by over 40%.

Senior Baker's Note:
Senior Bakers should be aware that federal regulations require proof of low-fat compliance on a half-yearly basis. You will have to work with your department buyers to maintain accurate records of the source of your ingredients.

Contents

Priority Level: *URGENT*

(The competition is expected to launch their own line

of fat-free éclairs any month now.)

The page below was printed in Acrobat Exchange using Adobe Serif and Adobe Sans.

Pastry Proposal: Exquisite Éclairs

The Experimental Kitchens Group

The following proposal is for a new line of fat-free frozen élairs (Exquisite Éclairs) to be marketed under the Nature's Gourmet product line. Research has shown that fat-free gourmet pastries will have a solid impact on the market place given today's health conscious consumer.

Our éclair recipes have been carefully researched to use existing stock ingredients, substituting butter with oil and using our own egg substitute. This should reduce the caloric content of the éclairs by 35% and the fat content by over 40%.

Senior Baker's Note:
Senior Bakers should be aware that federal regulations require proof of low-fat compliance on a half-yearly basis. You will have to work with your department buyers to maintain accurate records of the source of your ingredients.

Contents

Priority Level: *URGENT*
(The competition is expected to launch their own line of fat-free éclairs any month now.)

According to the US Department of Ordinance,
over 1 million memo grenades
are delivered every business day.

coffee^{break}

The memo grenade. Squabbles, fights, wars, feuds, power plays, reorganizations, positioning – they're what happens when people get together to work toward a single goal, whether you're in the Marines or the Kindergarten Teachers Association of New Jersey. It happens every day in every organization that employs people.

A memo grenade occurs when you throw the pin and keep the grenade. It is a document that you sometimes regret you wrote and almost always regret you sent. That note to your boss, the letter to the CEO, that searing commentary about salary standards – the little pinless bomb rocks merrily on the stepladder of your career while you fret about what will happen.

Everyone has either launched their own memo grenade at one time or another or has sighted one lobbed over office partitions and across org charts. If everybody just did their best and forgot about money, power, and control, the world would be a less explosive place to work and live. Unfortunately, memo grenades will exist as long as there is office communication.

Adobe Acrobat software can help reduce the cost of memo grenades. It can help speed the resolution of their contents with practically instantaneous delivery. If you must write memo grenades at least now you have the right tools and the delivery system to let that pin fly.

Recognize any of the examples on the following two pages?

Not every document is strictly business. If fact, there are plenty of documents out there that stand in the way of getting things done.

Let's take a break and look at the lighter side of how people sometimes miscommunicate.

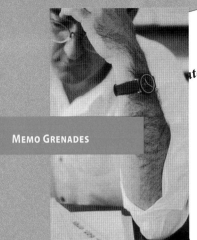

ate Interior Designs, Inc.
INTEROFFICE MEMORANDUM

To: Fred Barnard
From: Elaine Green
Re: Offices

It's been two years since you promised me a window office. I was just wondering whether you're still thinking about giving me one.

On the next page is a floor plan drawing. I've taken the liberty to show you where I'd like to sit.

I know you've been busy lately, but I'd like to remind you that I sit here all day in the dark confines of the inner office and I really do need more light to do my work. As you know I work a lot with color. The fluorescent lights make it all but impossible to do my work. And, after all, you promised to give me a office. I've been waiting for you to give me that office. Jeff down the hall got an office over a year ago. I thought that office was mine.

All the noise around here is distracting...

The Robinson Group

Memorandum

To: The Executive Staff
From: Tiffany Flail
Subject: Reorganization Plans

Don't you people ever think about how hard we work down here. There are employees who have given their whole lives to this company and now you simply move them from one organization to another without thought of how they feel. Several people were crying yesterday because they'll no longer be working together.

I think your reorganization plans have given little thought to how we work as a group. You've changed our lives, yet not one of you has come down here since you announced the re-org plans yesterday. No one is doing any work. I'm trying to hold the department together but it seems I'm the only one working at this company to do so.

On the next few pages are memos I've gotten from you remarking how well we work together. Please refresh your minds with your own words.

Either do something fast or not at all...I'm tired of all this interruption to my life...

Worldwide Financial Investments, Inc

Memorandum

To: Susan Nelson, Director of Operations
From: R. R. Donald
Re: Salary Adjustment

Dear Ms. Nelson:

I am sick and tired of accepting low wages for premium work. I have talked with several of my fellow workmates and all of them have remarked that, without exception, the work I do for the company is outstanding and exceptional. Yet I continue to work at a grade 87, when it's obvious that Bill Overpenny, who's work is not the same caliber as mine, is a grade 89. On the next two pages are a series of graphs and charts that show how my abilities excel over any one else's on your staff. Please take a look at them. (It took me over two days to get them right.)

This obvious lack of vision on the part of the Department of Operations will eventually lead me to resign and search for other work if you are not able to see my point of view.

you about this tomorrow. I'm busy on Wednesday iday I have a vacation day.

nent must stop. I'd like to talk to you about it.

GLOBAL INDUSTRIES
Interoffice Memorandum

To: John Smith, VP, Global Industries
From: Tim Golden
RE: Working With You

Thank you for your prompt payment for my consulting work. However, I do want to point out one thing: I had an extremely difficult time working with your staff managers. I found many of them to be slightly on the pompous side and they never really took my consulting advice seriously. I've enclosed complete details on the next 15 pages or so.

May I remind you that I have a MBA from Houston and a PhD from Ohio. Before National Industries laid me off last year, I had over 10 years experience doing what many of your managers do (but not very well).

Other than your staff managers, and how I think they helped to make my report a month late, it was a pleasure doing business with you. I'll call next week to see how my expertise can be put to better use for future projects.

Over 92 billion original documents
are created every year.

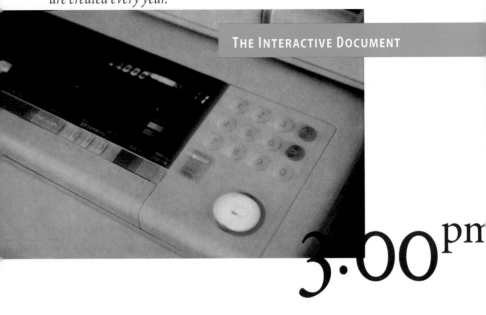

THE INTERACTIVE DOCUMENT

3.00^{pm}

Any corporation large enough to produce chocolate-frosted éclairs and fat-free camper food and sell them for a profit throughout the world is a big enterprise. Bythos Corporation has grown exponentially since its beginnings on the streets of Toronto, when Pierre and Fred worked side by side.

At corporate headquarters, which houses about 5,000 employees, getting to and from buildings is both confusing and time consuming. Employees constantly refer to their employee directory, a 100-page combination phone book, building directory, and conference room locator.

Published twice a year and sent to every employee via interoffice and regular mail, the employee directory requires a great deal of Marcia Zwerner's time in a remote corner of the Employee Relations department. Marcia works with HR, Facilities, and Employee Relations, and updates the employee directory's people, places, and organizations.

A recent survey of Bythos employees found that the Employee Directory does not serve its employees as well as it could. Marcia's marching orders are to address those concerns in the next Bythos Employee Directory (BED). Her meeting to outline her new strategy to her boss, James Matt, is about to begin.

At 15,000 employees in 55 buildings scattered over four continents, one of Bythos' biggest problems is employee communications: who is who, where do they sit, and how can I get information to them?

Each year 400 billion photocopies are produced
at an average cost of ½ cent per sheet.

The Interactive Document

Producing an effective Employee Directory can save thousands and thousands of employee hours that might be put to better use.

Marcia already knows what Mr. Matt wants or doesn't want:

----> No more dull, typewritten lists.

----> No more straining to find someone's building and country location.

----> No more phone calls to find someone's fax number and then having to wait a day for the voice mail reply .

----> No more having his secretary spend an hour trying to find the Vanilla Bean conference room.

----> No more employee surveys that tarnish the Employee Relations department.

Marcia asked for a personal computer and has painstakingly learned all the computer applications she will need to write, design, and produce the Employee Directory. Her meeting with Mr. Matt begins with showing sample artwork and sample pages.

First off, she tells Mr. Matt, her maps are now illustrated. Secondly, her phone list is arranged by last name then by a completely different first-name index. Next to each listing is the employee's building code, city, and country code, an abbreviated acronym of their department, and their phone and fax numbers.

Finally, she shows a wide array of organizational charts
that cover the entire corporation, all locations, and
all organizations. The org charts are color-coordinated
with the city and building locations. Marcia also put in
a troubleshooting guide for the phone system, HR, and
Employee Relations departments.

"There are two slight problems…" she begins. "If you want
color we will have to either color-copy it, or actually print
it. And the other is that the directory will be about
50 pages bigger, probably close to 150 pages. We'll still print
about 15,000 copies but we should have a few left over."

"How much?" Mr. Matt asks. "About 2¢ a page rather than
the normal 1¢," Marcia responds, "then about $3,000 more
to distribute the directory. Same as always."

Mr. Matt ponders for a bit and grudgingly approves the
costs. "How long?" he asks. Mr. Matt always says the
same three things: How Much? How Long? and Keep Me
Informed. Marcia explains that the color and added pages
will require more production time with every update,
maybe two or even three additional weeks.

Mr. Matt nods his head and clears his throat. Time for
Marcia to leave. As she exits Mr. Matt says, "Keep me informed, Marcia."

	2¢	per page for color
x	150 pages	
x	15,000 copies	
+	$3,000 to mail	
=	$48,000 x twice a year	
=	$96,000	

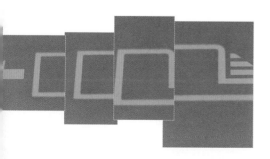

By 1996 total projected sales of laptop and notebook computers are expected to exceed 20 million units.

Adobe Acrobat software makes the networks of most businesses and corporations more efficient by seamlessly connecting diffuse computer systems, environments, and applications.

Most corporations have some sort of employee directory. The bigger the corporation the bigger the directory. Acrobat software enables Marcia to publish the Employee Directory in electronic form and distribute it over the existing network.

┈┈╴〉 Employees now can view *or* print it. If they choose to print, they can print one page, a number of pages, or the entire directory.

┈┈╴〉 Employees can have an electronic copy residing on their notebook computers for travel or at home on their home computers.

┈┈╴〉 Employees can maneuver through the 150 pages by using Bookmarks, Thumbnails, or by creating links.

┈┈╴〉 Employees can perform searches for specific names, meeting rooms, or any other text.

This type of material exists naturally on a network. Not only is it easily accessed in a Bythos building or a motel room in Tennessee, but Marcia can easily change and distribute the employee directory by upgrading the electronic copies on the Bythos network.

At some point, Bythos will put together all their internal publications and offer them together on a special network server. All the latest employee information can be kept there and constantly updated as needed.

Network access also means that people can download the entire directory and then manipulate the contents to suit their needs. Why deliver 150 pages of a directory to a person who only requires the Australian phone list? Using Acrobat Exchange, the information can be downloaded and unnecessary pages deleted, without losing the view or print options.

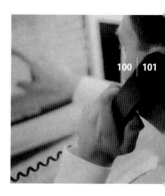

100 | 101

The savings of electronically publishing the Employee Directory over the Bythos network is considerable. The time and productivity savings is immediate. Marcia's plan integrates more than a phone directory. The Bythos employee directory is to be a source book for department listings, organizational charts, and building maps.

Marcia uses the Link Tool in Acrobat Exchange to create interactive links from one page to another. This gives her new source book a truly interactive feel. Any text or graphic can be linked to any other area in the document – from a small area to an entire page.

To create a link:

----⟩ Select the Link tool and designate the area that will become the link; you will connect this link to another view within the document.

Link Tool

----⟩ Move to the page to be linked. You can also use a particular magnification view for the linked page. Create the link.

The link is now connected to the selected view. Now any user who selects that linked area or text will go automatically to the designated area. Any user who receives the employee directory can create Links to suit their *own* jobs, place of employment, or general preferences.

The following four pages show a few sample pages from the Bythos Sourcebook. The same kind of interactive links can be put into any document, even including the dryest spreadsheet.

6,000 employees print the BED on their local printer

= $9,000x twice a year

= $18,000

----⟩ Acrobat savings of $ 74,000 !

Linking two objects together within an electronic document is not only easy but can be done very creatively. While the next four pages will illustrate one example, our Bythos Employee Directory, hundreds of examples are possible.

When using Acrobat Exchange or Acrobat Reader software, activate the link by selecting a "linked" area of the page (here signified by the colored buttons). Once activated the software will advance (or recede) to the appropriate page.

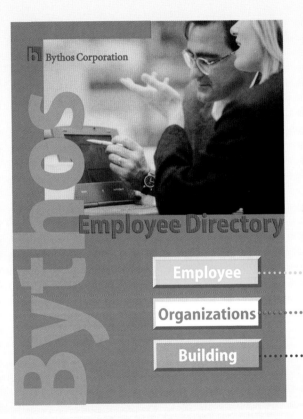

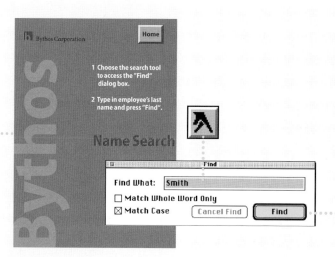

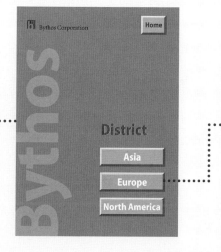

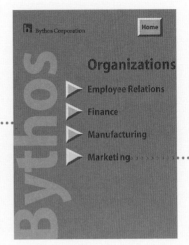

Organizations

- Employee Relations
- Finance
- Manufacturing
- Marketing

Germany

Berlin

Hannover

Münich

Münich

Building

Meeting Rm

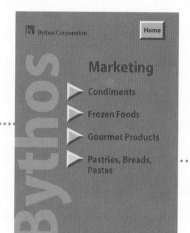

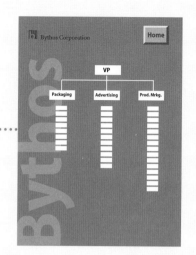

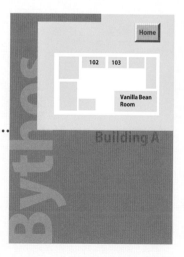

4:00^{pm}

As mobile computing continues to make technical advancements, the portable document is here today.

The world is becoming smaller and offices are becoming mobile as we can carry our notebook computers and modems into the streets and airports of the world. A worldwide network is just a phone away, and advances in remote access can link you to your office network even though you're on another continent.

Mobile computing is advancing faster than this small book could hope to describe but what is apparent is that your office is no longer the only place you can "work." Telecommuting from home to office is encouraged in many corporations. Frequent flyers swear they get more work done on the plane than anywhere else. Sales reps can now "download" and "upload" computer files from all over their territory or even during a sales call. Soon cellular technology will enable wireless mobile computing. The cafés of the world will never be quite the same.

Even if you're not "mobile," Adobe Acrobat technology is making the document "portable." CD-ROMs will replace printed encyclopedias. Documentation manuals will live on-line. Libraries will be able to share entire bookshelves over the phone line. The mobility and portability of information will take quantum leaps as microprocessors gain speed and storage capacity.

As this book has tried to suggest, the digital life of a PDF document far surpasses the paper one in scope, richness, and accessibility. The next several pages involve our last case study of the day. It's 4:00 pm and time to move beyond paper.

106 | 107

Adobe Acrobat technology will enable mobile users to view, share, access, and store documents of all kinds.

◄ *page 26*

► *page 116-117*

*Advancements in office technologies are changing
the way business is conducted.*

THE PORTABLE DOCUMENT

Robert Hernandez is about to make a sales call on Janice Hill. Robert is a regional sales rep for CubeWorks. Janice is a procurement manager for Bythos Corporation. After trading voice mail messages over the past few months, they discover they'll be in the same airport at the same time with an hour or so to spare. Why not meet?

Janice's plane arrives and Robert is waiting for her at the gate. They walk to the airport lounge, find a secluded table, and begin their meeting. Niceties pass and numbers begin to fly. Robert makes his pitch on CubeWorks' products. Janice discusses Bythos' future facilities needs.

The Presentation ····>

Robert asks Janice if she would like to see the CubeWorks product line. When she agrees, Robert lifts his Macintosh notebook computer from his briefcase, turns it on, and begins the presentation of CubeWorks' products using Acrobat software. The presentation, prepared by Jackson's marketing communications staff, adapts readily to Janice's questions.

The Interactive Document ····>

After a half hour, Janice is impressed enough to offer Robert a reciprocal look at Bythos and its employees. She turns on her PC laptop and accesses the PDF employee directory created with Acrobat software. She uses the organizational charts to help explain the organization of Bythos. During her talk Robert asks for various departmental contacts. Janice stops her presentation, searches for the employee's last name, and the employee list appears highlighting name, phone, fax, and location. Janice then returns to the organizational chart. Robert comments on the PDF employee handbook and how helpful it is to see an overview of such a large corporation.

When Janice asks Robert if CubeWorks' can provide specialized products for large corporations, Robert opens an outline of the CubeWorks contract with The Zeb Group investment firm. A CubeWorks product marketing manager named Jack worked with The Zeb Group to modify a new line of office cubicles to Zeb's exact specifications. Robert retrieves the marketing brochure saved as a PDF file and zooms in on the new cubicle designs.

⇐···· **The Product Proposal**

Janice prepares several standard Bythos PDF forms for Robert to complete and return to Janice; these will allow Janice to submit CubeWorks as an approved vendor. She renames each file so Robert will more readily understand them. Besides the vendor forms, there's a legal boilerplate, and a Bythos corporate backgrounder.

⇐···· **The Simple Document**

Janice then accesses the Bythos Sourcebook, deletes all the pages except the appropriate org chart of the Corporate Procurement Department and saves that as a new three-page PDF file. All the files are copied from her PC onto a diskette for Robert's notebook computer.

Robert, in turn, prepares a scaled-down version of his data sheet presentation. He customizes it by deleting several sections, and then inserts a one-page document he recently created and of which he is very proud: an electronic business card with his picture on it.

⇐···· **The Diverse Document**

When Janice gives him the diskette, he copies her files then puts his own files onto the diskette and hands it back. It's time to go. They close their notebook computers, shake hands, and leave with a feeling of accomplishment.

Information technology tools and new models of doing business will evolve together. What seems odd today will be taken for granted tomorrow.

When Robert boards his plane and begins his next flight, he reviews the material Janice gave him and starts to write several memos: one memo to his boss, one to CubeWorks legal, and several to members of the executive staff at CubeWorks. After composing each memo, he creates PDF files using the PDF Writer and puts the memos in his electronic "out" basket. Robert attaches the pertinent files Janice gave him onto each of the executive staff memos.

Mobile Computing ····⇢

Next he writes two or three letters of introduction to the Bythos contacts Janice gave him. Again he creates PDF files of the letters when he finishes writing them, and then attaches PDF marketing material and data sheets to each letter. He customizes the material for each letter.

When he arrives at his destination, Robert has dinner then returns to his hotel room to finish the day's work. Connecting his notebook computer to the phone in the room, he calls his office and accesses CubeWorks' E-mail system. He attaches the PDF memos to an E-mail message and sends the memos. Before logging off the modem connection, Robert makes a back-up copy of his memos and Janice's PDF files onto the remote server.

Remote Access of ····⇢
Portable Documents

The last item on Robert's to-do list is to send the letters and materials to his new Bythos contacts. For this, Robert makes a direct fax connection with his notebook computer via the modem. He opens each PDF document and faxes the material directly from Acrobat Exchange to the fax numbers Janice provided.

Faxing Portable ····⇢
Documents

All in all it's been a busy, but productive day. As Robert watches the late-night news he cannot contain his excitement about Bythos. If he lands this customer it will make The Zeb Group look like small potatoes.

The timely delivery of information is one of the new competitive measures of conducting business.

THE PORTABLE DOCUMENT

Interactive Documents ⋯⟩

Document Interchange ⋯⟩

Document Processing ⋯⟩

Janice exaggerated her departure time to Robert. It wasn't exactly a lie, she just wanted a little time to herself between flights. She sits comfortably in an airline executive club with a glass of wine. After a few minutes thinking about CubeWorks, Janice opens her notebook PC and starts the CubeWorks' PDF presentation that Robert prepared for her on his Macintosh notebook computer.

Maneuvering through the 80 or so products is easy and informative. Janice is impressed. She opens the company backgrounder and reads about CubeWorks. She likes the inventiveness of the company and their easy business style, and she likes Robert's electronic business card. Maybe Bythos *should* do business with this young company. Maybe some of their vitality will rub off on Bythos.

Janice decides to review the most recent financial statements of her department and opens a 15-page spreadsheet in PDF format. She searches for "cubicles" and finds the line on page 9. Amazingly, Bythos is spending more than 2 million dollars a year on office renovation, cubicle partitions, and office furniture. She opens another PDF file with last year's totals, completes the same search, and discovers that office renovation costs have risen 88 percent in the past year. She opens one last PDF file, a 200-page Bythos vendor report, and discovers that all office renovation is contracted through a single company, probably without competing bids.

Before Janice leaves the airport club she decides on a course
of action. On the plane she'll write a couple of memos to
her boss and to the buyer of office facilities recommending
that CubeWorks become an active bidder in their future
purchases. She'll include pages from the spreadsheets she
reviewed, and a few pages from Robert's material. Tomorrow, when she returns to the office, she'll send out her PDF
memos to her peers and staff.

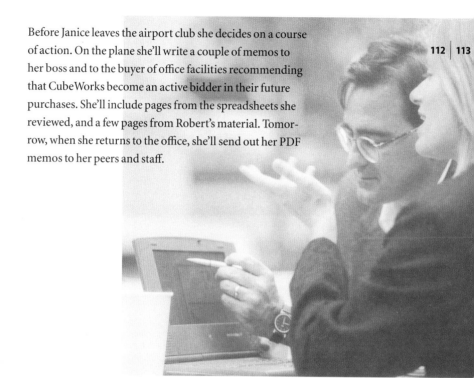

5:00^{pm}

In the very near future a set of tools for corporate and commercial publishers will provide a way to create PDF documents with a variety of enhanced functions. Publishers will use these tools to add value to PDF versions of their publications. Books, manuals, magazines, journals, even newspapers will be "published" electronically, either online or on CD-ROM.

Acrobat tools for publishers will enable automatic "live-linked" indexes for documents, allowing the reader to locate any text by selecting an index entry; users will instantly locate any word or entry in a document, or even cross-reference different subjects within a document or set of documents. Optical Character Recognition (OCR) technology will directly port scanned pages into PDF documents – a tremendous boon to libraries, publishers, and corporate archives.

Adobe is also working on the inclusion of audio and visual elements into PDF documents. Because they will be connected to something intimately familiar – the document – this promise will give real definition to the term multimedia.

Books and magazines of the future will be physically embodied in a computer with a high-resolution color screen that weighs less than a paper magazine. Such computers will contain the information from millions of pages and have electronic access to billions more.

Adobe Acrobat technology will address the needs of the many organizations that publish documents written in the Standard Generalized Markup Language (SGML), or other file formats, such as RTF (Rich Text Format). New Acrobat extensions and products will enable both document structure and appearance within a single PDF file by combining the native file and its structure with the corresponding PDF file; filters will identify the structure of numerous other file formats, such as Microsoft Word, WordPerfect, and FrameMaker. Automated links, structure-based full text searches, and other features, such as the ability to extract SGML from a "structured" PDF file, will give professional and commercial publishers all the benefits of electronic document exchange without losing document structure.

These and other technologies will ultimately change the economics of publishing. The physical constraints of paper and the associated restrictions of its delivery will eventually disappear. Information will still be printed, but it will no longer be a necessary step in the distribution process. In a few years it will cost less to deliver phone books to the entire country than it now costs to deliver them to one small town; it will cost less to deliver 10,000 color catalogs than it does today to deliver one; it will cost less to deliver all the business magazines than it does today to deliver a few sheets of paper.

This change in the economics of document delivery will transform the information business. The magazine will no longer be a single layer of information. Since numbers of advertising pages will not be directly related to the cost of delivery, it will be possible for magazines to have "deep" ads that contain innumerable product specifications.

The value of future documents will not be measured by today's standards. Since documents will include massive amounts of information (a magazine could easily be 10,000 pages long), success will depend on the user's ability to navigate. Feature articles might contain video and audio and enough background information to fill a full-length novel. Editorial content and interface design will have to rise to the occasion by providing information that allows the relating and amplifying of concepts and ideas.

In twenty years, we will have access to ever-widening circles of information. Millions of electronic pages will be readily available and complex searches on diverse material across multiple databases will be an everyday occurrence. Just as computers changed the way people create documents, computers will also change the way people communicate them, as well as the nature of the documents themselves. The world beyond paper is nearer than you might think.

glossary

Adobe Acrobat A family of retail products that allows users to send documents created on their computer to other computer users regardless of the hardware platform, operating system, or application software used to create the original. The document can be read, annotated, printed, and stored by the receiving computer.

Acrobat Distiller A software program that translates PostScript language files into PDF files.

Acrobat Exchange A software application that allows users to navigate, view, print, and create PDF documents. Available for DOS, Macintosh, UNIX, and Windows platforms, Acrobat Exchange is the full-feature communication application.

Acrobat Reader A software application allowing users to navigate, view, and print PDF documents. Available for DOS, Macintosh, UNIX, and Windows platforms, Acrobat Reader is the view and print only Acrobat application.

Adobe Systems Incorporated A developer of software technology for creating, displaying, and printing digital documents.

ASCII American Standard Code for Information Exchange. An internationally accepted standard for exchanging text information electronically. ASCII text is unformatted and communicates only character keystrokes.

Bookmarks A way to obtain an overview of a document within Acrobat Exchange or Acrobat Reader. Bookmarks electronically tag a page and a particular view within a PDF file. Names can be assigned to each Bookmark.

Document Information that uses one or more of the following elements for communication: type, graphics, photos, audio, video.

DOS Disk Operating System. While many computer systems have Disk Operating Systems, the popular use of it today refers to MS-DOS, or Microsoft DOS, as developed by Microsoft Corporation.

Electronic Document   A document that exists in electronic format as opposed to one that exists on paper.

E-mail   Electronic mail. A software application that allows computer users to communicate over a network. E-mail messages are transmitted as unformatted ASCII text, although many E-mail applications allow non-E-mail electronic files to be attached and transported from computer to computer.

EPS   Encapsulated PostScript. An EPS file has PostScript page description language information "embedded" into the file, allowing different and diverse software applications to share the file without disturbing the file's native attributes.

Font Substitution   PDF files carry information about the fonts used in a document without actually including the font. Acrobat technology substitutes a "master" font in its place to maintain the look and feel of the original document, be they viewed on a computer monitor or printed to paper.

LAN   Local Area Network. A computer network that is physically in one locality, such as a network connecting a department, a floor, or a building. Most networks are comprised of several LANs pieced together.

Macintosh   A family of personal computers from Apple Computer, Inc.

Memo Grenade   A memo that can backfire or explode, hence a memo in which you "throw the pin and keep the grenade."

PDF   *See* Portable Document Format.

PDF Writer   A specially designed printer driver that produces PDF files from applications. It is bundled with the Acrobat Exchange application for Macintosh and Windows environments. Not available for the UNIX and DOS platforms.

Portable Document	An electronic document that allows cross-platform, device independent transmission of its information.
Portable Document Format	The key to cross-platform functionality of Adobe Acrobat products is a unique PostScript language-based **120** | **121** file format. PDF is an open standard that Adobe Systems documents and publishes for use by software developers.
PostScript	A page description computer programming language that allows the creation, viewing, and printing of digital graphics and type. PostScript is licensed software available from Adobe Systems.
SGML	Standard Generalized Markup Language. A file format for document revision. With SGML, users "tag" a document's various elements before sending an ASCII file to an authoring application.
Thumbnails	A way to obtain an overview of a document within Acrobat Exchange or Acrobat Reader. Thumbnails show small pictures of individual pages.
UNIX	A computer operating system developed by AT&T (Bell Labs). There are dozens of UNIX variations that provide a basic set of UNIX operations on different hardware and software platforms.
WAN	Wide Area Network. A computer network that is geographically in different areas, such as two buildings, a campus of buildings, or a network stretching across the country or world by use of telecommunications lines. WANs are strung together of many Local Area Networks, or LANs. *See* LANs.
Windows	A software operating system that utilizes a graphic interface.

index

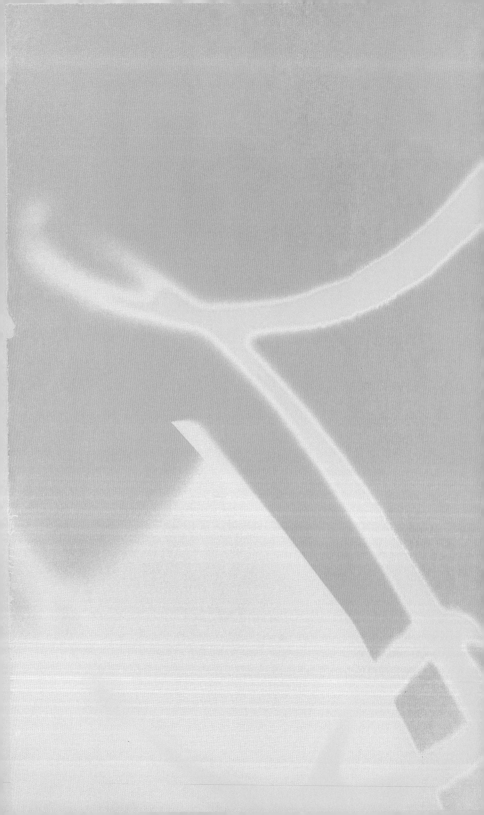

Design, illustration, and production

MetaDesign West, San Francisco, California.
Bill Hill, Terry Irwin, Andrew Waegel, Priska
Wollein, Nancy Zeches

Readers and advisors

Rob Babcock, Tim Bienz, Frank Boosman,
Debbie Hanna, Marj Hopper, Paul Klein, Clinton
Nagy, Linda Prosser, David Rogelberg, Mike Rose,
Judy Santoro, Deborah Triant, Roy Zitting

Editor

E.M. Ginger

Cover and text design

Priska Wollein

Photography

Kevin Ng

Designed and produced using Adobe Illustrator,
Adobe Photoshop, and QuarkXPress on Macintosh
IIci and Quadra computers.

Proofs were printed on an Apple LaserWriter IIg and
a Canon CLC 300 with an Adobe PostScript RIP.

Metagraphics, Palo Alto, California, created scans
and electronic duotones, and output final film
at 175 LPI using an Adobe/Scitex PostScript RIP and
Scitex Dolev imagesetter.

Typefaces from the Adobe Type Library were used
throughout this book, with Myriad and Minion
multiple master as primary text fonts.

Printed by Shepard Poorman, Indianapolis, Indiana.